Teaching with Empathy

Lisa Westman

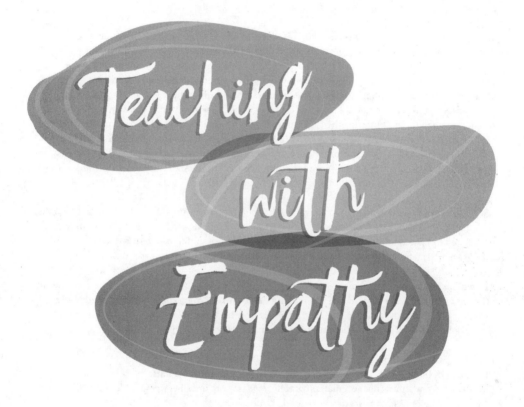

How to Transform Your Practice by
Understanding Your Learners

Alexandria, Virginia USA

1703 N. Beauregard St. • Alexandria, VA 22311-1714 USA
Phone: 800-933-2723 or 703-578-9600 • Fax: 703-575-5400
Website: www.ascd.org • Email: member@ascd.org
Author guidelines: www.ascd.org/write

Ranjit Sidhu, *CEO & Executive Director;* Penny Reinart, *Chief Impact Officer;* Genny Ostertag, *Senior Director, Acquisitions & Editing;* Julie Houtz, *Director, Book Editing;* Mary Beth Nielsen, *Editor;* Thomas Lytle, *Creative Director;* Donald Ely, *Art Director;* Georgia Park, *Senior Graphic Designer;* Valerie Younkin, *Senior Production Designer;* Cynthia Stock, *Typesetter;* Kelly Marshall, *Production Manager;* Shajuan Martin, *E-Publishing Specialist;* Christopher Logan, *Senior Production Specialist*

PAPERBACK ISBN: 978-1-4166-3048-7   ASCD product #121027   n8/21
PDF E-BOOK ISBN: 978-1-4166-3049-4; see Books in Print for other formats.
Quantity discounts are available: email programteam@ascd.org or call 800-933-2723, ext. 5773, or 703-575-5773. For desk copies, go to www.ascd.org/deskcopy.

Library of Congress Cataloging-in-Publication Data

Names: Westman, Lisa, author.
Title: Teaching with empathy : how to transform your practice by
    understanding your learners / Lisa Westman.
Description: Alexandria, Virginia : ASCD, 2021. | Includes bibliographical
    references and index.
Identifiers: LCCN 2021018990 (print) | LCCN 2021018991 (ebook) | ISBN
    9781416630487 (paperback) | ISBN 9781416630494 (pdf)
Subjects: LCSH: Affective education. | Empathy.
Classification: LCC LB1072 .W47 2021 (print) | LCC LB1072 (ebook) | DDC
    370.15/34—dc23
LC record available at https://lccn.loc.gov/2021018990
LC ebook record available at https://lccn.loc.gov/2021018991

30 29 28 27 26 25 24 23 22   2 3 4 5 6 7 8 9 10 11 12

*Dedicated to all the children in our classrooms
and the inner children within ourselves.*

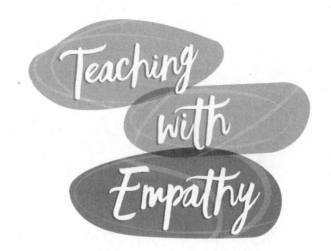

Preface..ix

Acknowledgments xiii

1. The Empathy Crisis 1

2. The Intersection of Empathy and Curriculum 13

3. The Empathetic Learning Environment.. 22

4. Empathy and Equity 43

5. Empathetic Instruction and Assessment Strategies 63

6. Empathetic Grading and Reporting Practices............................... 87

7. Where Do You Go from Here? Actionable Steps to Become
   a More Empathetic Educator...104

References 111

Index 115

About the Author 119

Preface

I began this project in August of 2019. At that time, I was profoundly curious about empathy and its role in teaching and learning. This was before the COVID-19 pandemic, before the Black Lives Matter protests sparked by the vicious murder of George Floyd, and before the swings of the 2020 U.S. presidential election and its aftermath swept our nation and the world.

I always had my "why" for writing this book, but the events of 2020 accelerated my curiosity and my conviction that what we need most in the world, and in the field of education specifically, is empathy. We need genuine empathy, not rhetoric, not feigned compassion, not pity—true empathy. My goal and greatest hope are that this book clarifies empathy—what it is and what it looks like in a learning environment—and serves as inspiration for you to continue to hone your empathy skills.

Learning about empathy is not always comfortable or easy. In fact, as I conducted my research for this book, I often felt poorly for some of my past actions (personal and professional). I recognized that I had acted without intentionally trying to empathize with others. I wish I could go back and do over many a conversation I had or decision I made. I anticipate that, as you read this book, you too may have feelings of regret. To this, I say that we must have compassion for ourselves and look forward. To paraphrase the great poet Maya Angelou, you do the best you can at the time, and then when you know better, you do better (Winfrey, 2011).

Why This Book?

Mental health and social-emotional learning (SEL) are two of the hottest topics in education right now. This is not a coincidence. The number of students in our classrooms who have experienced trauma is increasing (over half of 17-year-olds report experiencing trauma [Brackett, 2019]). Depression and anxiety rates are growing (approximately one in five U.S. children claim these conditions [Brackett, 2019]), and incidents of teen suicide are the highest they have been since World War II (Ducharme, 2019).

There is an empathy crisis in our world, according to journalist Maia Szalavitz and psychiatrist Bruce D. Perry (2010), and if we don't act individually and collectively to hone our empathy skills, they could become extinct. "For many children," says Mark Brackett (2019) of the Yale Center for Emotional Intelligence, "school might be the only place any of these issues are recognized and addressed" (p. 192). As educators, we have a great opportunity and responsibility to respond, and we must respond appropriately.

I am concerned that the education field's response to this crisis is much the same as with any previous hot topic: commercialize and mandate. Schools and districts make a plethora of boxed curricular tools and web-based "solutions" available to teach K–12 students social-emotional skills and facilitate learning about their mental health, and teachers are asked to teach one more content area. Instead, empathetic classrooms should be the foundation of learning—not the topic *du jour*.

We miss the mark with the same old model because it's not about what we do with the 30 minutes of SEL instruction or the curricular tool we adopt. It is about our day-to-day planning and our persona. Although 30 minutes of instruction certainly won't harm students, what we really need to be doing is focusing on a skill that we often overlook and undervalue: our own ability to empathize with others.

Why This Book Is for You

Educators' primary role in today's educational landscape is to ensure students feel safe and connected in a consistently empathetic learning environment. From our conversations with students to planning and delivering instruction, every action we take signifies our empathy level toward our students, colleagues, and ourselves. Many of us believe we are already empathetic to our students and their stories, but our actions, even unintentional, can implicitly shame students, compounding the disconnection they (and we) often feel.

As you will read about in Chapter 1, the opposite of empathy is shame— and repeated exposure to shame is a form of trauma (Tull, 2020). Regrettably, shame is inflicted on us and by us more frequently than most of us realize—a behavior I hope this book will help recognize and curb. We must assume, therefore, that all learners (children and adults) have experienced or are experiencing some type of trauma in their lives. Whether this is acute trauma (e.g., a parent dying) or ongoing traumas (e.g., an emotionally abusive parent; neglect; fear of repercussions because of race, religion, sexual orientation), we all will benefit and flourish when we are treated with empathy. The first step, while it may sound quite simplistic, is just recognizing that we are all human.

So, rather than try to identify who *needs* empathy, we start with the premise that all learners *deserve* empathy because it is crucial for any learning or growth to occur. This book will guide you to understand more, feel better, be more effective, and be more inspired. As a result, your students will feel the same way. You will learn to stop blaming students for perceived shortcomings and yourself for students you were unable to reach. Instead, we'll replace these feelings of blame and shame with compassion and acceptance.

Thank you for choosing to come along with me on this journey toward building your collective empathy. Happy reading!

Acknowledgments

I am eternally grateful for the people who knowingly or unknowingly influenced this book by sharing their stories and expertise with me.

Thank you to all of the teachers who invited me into their classrooms, administrators who invited me into their schools and districts, and students who invited me into their worlds. A special thank you to Enrique Castro; Cathy Fisher; Dr. Carol Kelly; Kellie Ringel; Stefanie Rothstein; Honowai Elementary School in Waipahu, Hawaii; The Otus Team; and the 2nd grade team (in particular, Lydia Florez, Sandy Hathaway, Sue Jaffe, Cathy Krupp, Katie Markowski, Theresa Sterner, and Thatcher Tong) at Holmes Primary School in Clarendon Hills, Illinois, for your valuable contributions to this book.

Thank you to my incredibly empathetic and astute editors at ASCD, Mary Beth Nielsen and Genny Ostertag. I am so grateful for all of your guidance and expertise.

Thank you to Carol Ann Tomlinson and members of the Empathetic Schools group who pushed my thinking on this topic and all things education.

Most of all, thank you to my greatest inspirations and support: Keith, Keller, Mallory, Darci, and Diesel. I love you all.

1

The Empathy Crisis

If you search "empathy and education," Google returns more than 73 million results, including an abundance of articles, blog posts, tweets, memes, and more. Of these results, more than 4 million are specific to empathy and the 2020 school closures caused by the COVID-19 pandemic, with an outpouring of pleas to "have empathy," "be empathetic," "get through this crisis with empathy." I clicked on dozens of my search results to get a sense of how empathy is portrayed. Many of these appeals hit me right in the gut; I could feel how earnest educators were in their efforts to do right by kids.

Other times the word *empathy* was used, though, I felt confused. At first, I wasn't 100 percent sure why I felt so unsettled, but then it hit me: for many of the results, empathy was a directive like "please have empathy." If it were as easy as just saying it, we would all be more empathetic. But there is much more to being empathetic than someone telling us to be that way.

This chapter will give an overview of what empathy is, what it looks like, and what is detrimental to empathic capacity as you work to ensure your schools are holistically empathetic learning environments. Before you read any further, consider completing the empathy pre-assessment, the personal self-reflection, and the educators' empathy checklist in Figures 1.1–1.3 to test your working knowledge of empathy and its intersection with education. The answers to the pre-assessment are at the end of this chapter, and you will also have a chance to retake it at the end of the book to see how your understanding grows.

FIGURE 1.1 **Empathy Assessment**		
(Answers are listed at the end of the chapter.)		
1.	There are three different types of empathy.	❏ True ❏ False
2.	Empathy is a personality trait.	❏ True ❏ False
3.	*"I feel so sorry for them"* is an empathetic statement.	❏ True ❏ False
4.	Empathy and sympathy are received by people in the same way.	❏ True ❏ False
5.	Empathy can be explicitly or implicitly conveyed.	❏ True ❏ False
6.	*"I can imagine you are feeling a variety of emotions right now"* is an empathetic statement.	❏ True ❏ False
7.	Empathy is a skill that must be practiced intentionally.	❏ True ❏ False
8.	In the absence of empathy, shame often results.	❏ True ❏ False
9.	Shame motivates humans to change their behaviors.	❏ True ❏ False
10.	Humans can grow their empathic capacity.	❏ True ❏ False

FIGURE 1.2 **Empathy Self-Reflection**
I can correctly identify my own feelings. ❏ Yes ❏ No
Which statement describes you better? ❏ I am comfortable with experiencing a range of emotions: happy, sad, excited, angry, frustrated. ❏ There are certain emotions (sad, scared, excited) that I am not comfortable experiencing.
When other people are sad, I . . . ❏ Try to make them feel better ❏ Listen to them
On a scale of 1–5, how comfortable are you asking other people questions about their feelings? **0**   **1**   **2**   **3**   **4**   **5** ◄───► Not comfortable at all; I don't want to pry.   Extremely comfortable; I do it all of the time.
I am aware of my implicit biases. ❏ Yes ❏ Somewhat ❏ No ❏ I do not have any implicit biases.

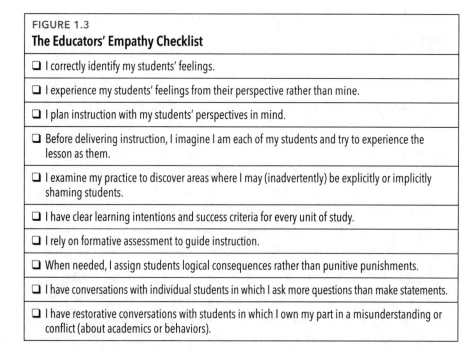

FIGURE 1.3
The Educators' Empathy Checklist

❑ I correctly identify my students' feelings.

❑ I experience my students' feelings from their perspective rather than mine.

❑ I plan instruction with my students' perspectives in mind.

❑ Before delivering instruction, I imagine I am each of my students and try to experience the lesson as them.

❑ I examine my practice to discover areas where I may (inadvertently) be explicitly or implicitly shaming students.

❑ I have clear learning intentions and success criteria for every unit of study.

❑ I rely on formative assessment to guide instruction.

❑ When needed, I assign students logical consequences rather than punitive punishments.

❑ I have conversations with individual students in which I ask more questions than make statements.

❑ I have restorative conversations with students in which I own my part in a misunderstanding or conflict (about academics or behaviors).

What Exactly Is Empathy?

Author, researcher, and social worker Brené Brown, one of the world's leading experts on empathy, defines the term as "the skill or ability to tap into our own experiences in order to connect with an experience someone is relating" (2007, p. 33). Textbook authors Allen Ivey, Paul Pederson, and Mary Ivey (2001, as cited in Brown, 2007) also define empathy as "the ability to perceive a situation from another person's perspective. To see, hear and feel the unique world of the other" (p. 33).

Although these definitions are straightforward and clear, empathy remains widely misunderstood, and our assessment of our own ability to take the perspectives of others is often skewed (Szalavitz & Perry, 2010, p. 1). Contrary to popular belief, empathy is not something people are born with or without. Instead, empathy is a skill that we are born with the *capacity to demonstrate*, but like all skills, it must be cultivated and continually sharpened.

Empathy is also multifaceted, comprising three different types: affective, cognitive, and behavioral.

Affective empathy is feeling what others are feeling; this is the emotional part of empathy. We sense that someone is sad, and we mirror their response and feel sad in return. For example, when we see someone else cry, we may cry in return. We will feel the sadness the other person feels.

Reflect: What emotions are you most able to feel? Why? What emotions are most difficult for you to feel? Why?

Try This: For one week, keep a journal of your interactions with other people (e.g., friends, family, colleagues). When you interact, note the other person's feelings. Then, write down how you knew the person felt this way (i.e., was it their tone of voice, facial expression, something they said?).

Cognitive empathy is the perspective-taking component: recognizing that other people have thoughts and feelings separate from our own. We go beyond feeling what a person is feeling and try to step into that person's shoes. We ask ourselves, "What might it feel like to be sad under the circumstances another person feels sad? What factors contribute to this person's experience of this feeling? How might this differ from my experience?"

Reflect: Think of an example of when you have demonstrated cognitive empathy. How did your perspective differ from another's perspective?

Try This: Continue with your journaling. Indicate how your perspective of the situation played a role. Did you think about what you would do if you were the other person? Or did you think about what you would do in their situation as *you*? Now, jot down what additional factors this person has to incorporate into their decision making (e.g., gender, age, race). How might these factors influence their perspective?

Behavioral empathy (also referred to as empathic concern) is what prompts us to act. This is when we feel, take on another perspective, and are driven to respond (Riess, 2018). It is what causes us to stand up to bullies when someone else is the victim. It is what informs how we vote in elections. This is our call to action.

Reflect: How often do you seek to understand your students' feelings and perspectives before planning instruction?

Try This: Engage in a conversation with a student and tally the number of questions you ask versus statements you make. Did you make more statements or ask more questions? The next time you chat with a student, ask a question when you feel like making a statement. Note the difference in your understanding of this student's perspective when you ask more questions.

In terms of planning instruction for students, our goal is to consistently and intentionally exhibit empathy that falls somewhere in between cognitive and behavioral. You may be wondering why we wouldn't always aim for behavioral empathy. The reason is that some professions (e.g., health care workers, social workers, teachers, police officers) are predisposed to something called "compassion fatigue" simply by the sheer number of exposures to the feelings and experiences (often tragic in nature) of others. It is (sadly) impossible to act on every empathic impulse, and acting isn't always appropriate; sometimes, genuine understanding is more suitable. Educators must strike a balance between thinking and acting—or better yet, *thinking before acting*—in the proactive approach that we consistently take to ensure we are educating students in an empathetic learning environment. Chapters 2–7 illustrate the proactive measures we can take with stories, examples, and ideas.

What Does Empathy Look Like?

Demonstrating empathy has physical markers as well as cerebral attributes. How we stand, our facial expressions, our tone of voice, and more can indicate the depth of our empathic capacity to others.

Have you ever watched someone feed a baby and noticed that the person feeding the baby opens his or her mouth just as the baby does when it eats the spoonful of food? This is an example of mirror neurons at work. Mirror neurons are a relatively new discovery (by neuroscientist Giacomo Rizzolatti and Vittorio Gallese at the University of Parma in Italy in the 1990s). How large a role mirror neurons play in empathy lacks consensus by scientists and doctors, but they do agree that mirror neurons exist and are activated when we feel something that others are experiencing (Marsh, 2012).

Mirror neurons also play a role in how we perceive others. Although mirror neurons allow us to feel what others feel and sometimes mimic what other people do, they don't automatically result in identical behaviors. For instance, if I am watching a horror movie, my mirror neurons allow me to feel scared for the protagonist, even though I am not personally in danger. My response to feeling afraid for this other person's plight is to hide under a blanket. Someone else's response might be to turn off the movie. If my friend shares that she is terrified of a stalker in a real-life situation, my mirror neurons cause me to feel scared, just like she does. I am so frightened that I am not conscious of the look on my face or that I'm anxiously tapping my foot on the ground. My mirror neurons may allow me to feel what another is feeling, but how I respond physically may or may not be empathetic.

The majority of what we communicate is nonverbal; some experts say up to 93 percent (Thompson, 2011). To demonstrate empathy, therefore, we must note what our bodies are saying, as well as our words. Helen Riess, a clinical psychiatry professor at Harvard Medical School, identified seven keys to nonverbal empathetic behavior based on the acronym EMPATHY (see Figure 1.4). These keys help us to be mindful of not only our own nonverbal cues but also others' nonverbal cues to better understand their perspective.

FIGURE 1.4
Nonverbal Empathy Checklist

Eye contact	Making an appropriate amount of eye contact
Muscles	Examining facial expressions, smiles, eyebrow raises, biting lips
Posture	Noticing stance: standing up straight or not, crossing or opening our arms
Affect	Feeling and acknowledging an emotion
Tone of voice	Adjusting the volume, pace, and rhythm of our speech
Hearing	Listening to another person, paying attention and responding without judgment
Your response	Not your verbal response—your feeling. How does another person's experience make you feel?

Source: Adapted from *Empathy effect: Seven neuroscience-based keys for transforming the way we live, love, work, and connect across differences* (pp. 45–58), by H. Riess (with L. Neporent), 2018, Boulder, CO: Sounds True, Inc.

Reflect: Think of someone you regard as not empathetic. What are their nonverbal cues like? Now, think of someone you regard as empathetic. What are their nonverbal cues like?

Try This: Make a video recording of yourself engaging in conversation with a small group of students. Then, watch the video and use the data collection tool from Figure 1.5 to tally your nonverbal interaction with students. If you're comfortable, partner with your instructional coach on this to get an extra set of eyes on your current nonverbal communication status and set a goal to increase your effectiveness.

FIGURE 1.5
Video Observation Data Collection Tool

Look Fors	Tone of Voice	Body Language	Facial Expressions
	Inviting: *patient, slow rate of speech* **Stopping:** *quicker pace of speech, sarcastic*	**Inviting:** *open hands, nodding head, sitting or standing at level with students* **Stopping:** *fisted hands, pointing fingers, walking away, crossing arms*	**Inviting:** *smiling, making direct eye contact, tilting head, nodding* **Stopping:** *frowning, grimacing, looking away, staring directly in someone's eyes*
Student #1			
Student #2			
Student #3			

So Why Is There an Empathy Crisis?

In their book *Born for Love: Why Empathy Is Essential—and Endangered*, authors Maia Szalavitz and Bruce Perry (2010) assert a variety of reasons they fear empathy is in danger, including the rise of technology use, the changing ways people co-exist, and decreasing community involvement. Additionally, we must acknowledge several natural barriers to exemplifying empathy that we then must actively work to compensate for as individuals.

For example, all of us are born with the ability to develop empathy, but we are *not* born automatically knowing how to empathize. Empathy is both a skill and an attribute. We must empathize (*skill*) to be empathetic (*attribute*). Like learning to speak, empathy is best developed through implicit connection and explicit modeling by our parents or close caregivers from the moment we are born. For various reasons, many children (and adults) have underdeveloped empathy skills, but it is never too late to learn, and recent research supports a correlation between the desire to become more empathetic and the ability to do so (Weisz, Ong, Carlson, & Zaki, 2020).

Furthermore, though we are born with the ability to empathize, we are also born with the instinct to protect ourselves from anything perceived as a threat. Sometimes, either because of external influences (like portrayals of people in the media) or because our own feelings get mixed up with others' feelings and we don't have the time or ability to reflect, we go into protection mode instead of empathizing.

Reflect: How would you describe your own capacity for empathy? What was your experience with empathetic caregivers in your childhood?

Try This: Journal about a specific memory that comes to mind when you reflect on these questions.

Although we have the ability to empathize with any and all humans, we are wired to empathize most with those who are similar to us (e.g., same gender, race, religion). This is called "in-group" bias. In-group bias has evolutionary roots; our ancestors lived in tribes as a means of survival for thousands of years.

Today, for much of the world, tribes are a thing of the past. Many of us live in diverse communities, and we are cognitively aware that the world is made up of innumerable types of people. Yet, biologically speaking, our brains are wired to feel more empathy when interacting with people like us.

Humans frequently "out-group" others without even recognizing we have done so (Riess, 2018, p. 33). We often don't even think about them as discrete groups, or we have become desensitized to the humanity of others, such as people suffering from addiction, obesity, or mental illnesses like hoarding or obsessive-compulsive disorder. Ironically, reality TV shows about the lives of these groups of people have become highly popular, which continually leads me to wonder whether these shows result in increased empathy for—or shaming of—the plights of others.

 Reflect: What group of people might you "out-group"? What "out-groups" do you belong to?

 Try This: Note any habits or activities you engage in that may be unconsciously perpetuating "othering" groups of people different than you. Can you give any of these up?

Shame Cannibalizes Empathy for Everyone

Shame, as defined by *Merriam-Webster,* is "a painful emotion caused by the consciousness of [toxic] guilt, shortcoming, or impropriety," and it is one of the most debilitating conditions we face. Feeling shame is so unbearable that the mere threat of shame is often exploited and weaponized as a means to control others and ourselves.

Sometimes the causes of shame are things that we are born with, but society can also assign or apply a "shortcoming" to things like race, religion, and gender. Some of us are literally born into a society that shames us just for being born. What the Black Lives Matter movement represents is an excellent example of this phenomenon in action on a large scale. The fact that this movement even exists is evidence of a critical lack of empathy and perpetuation of shame. This is because shame is rooted in judgment. Society teaches us to judge both others and ourselves.

We unconsciously, yet frequently, judge others to make ourselves feel better about ourselves or to make ourselves feel better about someone else's pain. Often our attempts to empathize with others can have the opposite result: we make them feel more ashamed. In *I Thought It Was Just Me (But It Isn't)*, Brené Brown (2007) outlines the concept of shame as the kryptonite of empathy. "Shame is the intensely painful feeling or experience of believing we are flawed and therefore unworthy of acceptance and belonging" (p. 5). A sense of belonging is crucial for people to be able to learn and grow.

We can, however, take steps to increase our ability to empathize rather than inadvertently shame. This is not easy, and it is not comfortable—and the process is ongoing. We may have greater shame resilience from some of our triggers than others. Brown (2007) outlines four criteria to help determine one's own shame resilience and allow for more empathy and less negative (yet natural) reactions (e.g., blame, aggression, defensiveness, and judgment) to shame:

1. Recognize and understand one's shame triggers.
2. Practice high levels of critical awareness of how systems and society shape our shame.
3. Be willing to reach out to others.
4. Possess the ability to speak shame.

When we experience shame, it is challenging to feel anything beyond fear, anger, and blame. To complicate matters, depending on our shame resilience level, which is fluid rather than constant, and our ability to appropriately identify our emotions, we may not even be conscious that what we feel is shame. We just *react*. We feel so badly that we engage in another seemingly unrelated or counterproductive manner to make the pain go away or make someone else feel as bad as we do (Brown, 2007, p. 67).

This is part of the reason why shame is so insidious. Take, for example, the student who is sent to the principal's office for goofing around in class. On his way, the student gets in a fistfight. Initially, one may conclude that the student lacks self-control or chooses to be defiant. But really, he was in a shame spiral. Now, a trip to the principal's office is elevated to an in-school suspension, increasing the shame the student experiences.

What if I add additional context to this story? Fifteen minutes before the teacher initially sent that student to the principal's office, that same principal had completed an unannounced walk-through at the exact moment the teacher sat down at her desk for the first time in hours. To the teacher, the principal's facial expression said, "I'm disappointed."

Depending on the teacher's own shame resilience, it is certainly possible that the teacher felt great shame during this walk-through because she felt imperfect or not valued. This feeling of shame based on judgment can exacerbate and displace one's reactions, hence her decision to send her student to the principal's office for wasting time.

Shame Begets Shame; Empathy Begets Empathy

Teachers, administrators, and the school system in and of itself can mitigate shame and foster empathy as means to remedy the empathy crisis in a variety of ways, as detailed in the remainder of this book. Perhaps, most important, educators have the unique opportunity to shape future generations of empathetic humans. Authors Marc Brackett (2019), Helen Riess (2018), and Maia Szalavitz and Bruce Perry (2010) each share a significant fact in their books on empathy: Although parents serve as the primary source of connection and influence for children, any consistent and stable adult can serve as a model of empathy and restore children's damaged bonds.

By the sheer number of hours students spend in school, schools (mainly teachers) have the most significant opportunity to serve this role. Responsive relationships between adults (teachers) and children (students) are mutually beneficial to both parties because they promote healthy childhood development (compensating for some of the trauma or toxic stress students experience elsewhere in their lives) and strengthen adults' core life skills (Center on the Developing Child at Harvard University, 2017).

We begin this process by being vulnerable, taking a critical look at our professional and organizational practices, and starting to replace practices rooted in shame with methods rooted in compassion. The following chapters will examine these approaches to teaching and learning.

Recommended Readings on Empathy

This chapter is far from an extensive analysis of empathy. If you would like to do a deeper dive into any of these elements, I recommend the following books:

Brown, B. (2007). *I thought it was just me (But it isn't)*. New York: Gotham.

Riess, H. (with Neporent, L.). (2018). *Empathy effect: Seven neuroscience-based keys for transforming the way we live, love, work, and connect across differences*. Boulder, CO: Sounds True, Inc.

Szalavitz, M., & Perry, B. D. (2010). *Born for love: Why empathy is essential—and endangered*. New York: Harper Paperbacks.

Zaki, J. (2019). *The war for kindness: Building empathy in a fractured world*. New York: Crown.

Figure 1.1 Empathy Assessment Answer Key
1. T; 2. F; 3. F; 4. F; 5. T; 6. T; 7. T; 8. T; 9. F; 10. T

2

The Intersection of Empathy and Curriculum

In his book *The Formative Five: Fostering Grit, Empathy, and Other Success Skills Every Student Needs,* Thomas Hoerr (2017) points out that schools have a duty to model and explicitly teach a multitude of emotional intelligence skills (at least one for every letter of the alphabet, he says). Hoerr narrows that list to the five most important skills and identifies empathy as the place to start. "In the absence of kindness and caring," Hoerr stresses, "relationships are destined to fail" (p. 37). He references the infamous Milgram experiment, where study participants were tested as to whether they would obey an authority figure and perform tasks that went against their conscience. Hoerr cites this experiment, which rather surprisingly showed that the subjects would continue to "shock" participants on the orders of the authority figure, as an example of how lack of empathy from a teacher results in cruelty to the learners. He believes that these types of situations are not limited to social experiments. They exist in our classrooms, too (Hoerr, 2016). It is crucial, therefore, to start the instructional process with empathy.

In the classroom, teachers frequently do not practice empathy as a proactive measure. It is more likely reactive: we feel with someone when they share their stories with us, or we can see on their faces that they are feeling a certain way. Genuine empathy, however, is demonstrated both explicitly (how we respond to a student) and implicitly (how we plan curriculum, instruction, assessment, and extracurricular learning opportunities).

"When we feel genuine empathy for a person," says Carol Ann Tomlinson (2021) in her latest book, *So Each May Soar,* "that affects our sense of responsibility for the person's welfare, how we think of them, how we listen to them, how we speak to them, and how we interact with them. It also influences our willingness to learn from them and to invest in them. Action informed by the world a child sees and knows can be quite different from action based in our own experiences" (p. 47).

Implicitly empathizing with students in the instructional planning process is a crucial component to demonstrating our compassion for students. Planning instruction without intention is more likely to result in students learning *shame* than the desired skill or content. Students are always learning; empathetic instructional planning helps to ensure students learn our intended objectives rather than unintentional and potentially scarring lessons. To further illustrate this point, consider the following two examples.

Kellie's Story

In the summer of 2019, while facilitating a professional development workshop on differentiation for a group of K–12 teachers in Illinois, I posed a question to participants that produced an answer I wasn't quite expecting. "Think of a time when you received particularly *unhelpful* feedback. What made the feedback unhelpful, and why?"

First, I had participants share their answers with their small groups. While I was circulating the room listening to various groups' responses, I saw the shocked expressions on the faces of one teacher's groupmates, and my interest was piqued. I walked over and asked this teacher, Kellie, to share her story with me and then if she was comfortable sharing with the whole group. She agreed. I paused the large group's conversation, and Kellie came to the front of the room and brought us back to her senior year in high school.

Kellie told us about an assignment she had in her English class that year: write a eulogy. The timing was uncanny for Kellie because her grandmother had just passed away two weeks earlier, and Kellie delivered the eulogy. She decided, therefore, to turn in the actual eulogy she gave for her grandmother. Then, Kellie dropped a bombshell on us: the grade she received for this eulogy assignment was a C–. Kellie was astonished and immediately asked her teacher, "Why did I get a C–?"

Kellie's teacher replied, "Your eulogy didn't resonate *with me.*"

To which Kellie responded, "I delivered that eulogy two weeks ago at my grandmother's funeral, and it really resonated with her family and friends."

And Kellie's teacher said, "Well, . . . it didn't resonate with me." And the grade stuck. Kellie was devastated. She remembers feeling deeply hurt and ashamed.

Now, Kellie was also a bright and innovative young lady. At the time, she also happened to be taking a course at her local community college, and she turned in that same eulogy to her college professor and received an *A*.

It was at that moment that Kellie said she learned three things:

1. Grades are not objective.
2. Grades are a form of shame for many students.
3. Students' feelings or feedback are not always considered in school.

Kellie doubts that any of these items were her teacher's actual learning targets for this class.[1]

Family Tree

Kellie's experience took place in 1999, so you may be thinking, "These days, stories like hers are less likely." If so, I encourage you to consider this second example, which took place in 2019.

My brother-in-law, Stephen, is a gay, single father in Chicago raising three incredible black boys—Jamarion, Jaylen, and Jacob. It's a nontraditional family structure that is becoming less unique with passing time. So, imagine Stephen's surprise when one day, his 1st grader, Jaylen, brings home the family tree assignment shown in Figure 2.1.

Jaylen would never be able to complete this assignment as outlined. Furthermore, Stephen (and I) wondered what the learning intentions even were.

Of course, no teacher sets out to discriminate or shame a student (an inherent display of lack of empathy) (Brown, 2007, p. 32). But if a teacher doesn't take steps to avoid these instances proactively, they will keep occurring. When we experience shame, it renders us unable to learn, so if school is about learning and growing, we cannot afford for this to continue. If we think of how much time, effort, and funding we put into our (often ineffective) reactive approaches (e.g., interventions, special education), we ought to refocus this time and energy into proactive approaches instead.

---

[1]A version of this example also appeared in the August 2020 issue of the ASCD newsletter *Education Update*.

FIGURE 2.1
Family Tree

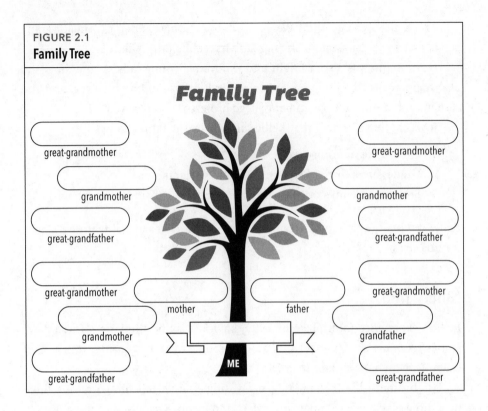

How Teacher Clarity Engenders Empathy

My previous book, *Student-Driven Differentiation: 8 Steps to Harmonize Learning in the Classroom* (Westman, 2018), illustrates eight proactive steps teachers can take to ensure all students learn, grow, and achieve. In short, student-driven differentiation shifts the focus from what students *do* (write a eulogy, create a family tree) to what students *learn* (write an emotionally compelling narrative, determine connections between the past and the present). Step one of student-driven differentiation is "Define learning intentions and success criteria with your grade-level and/or department-level colleagues" (Westman, 2018, p. 60). It is here where the roots of empathetic learning experiences are planted.

Author John Hattie (2012) discusses learning intentions and success criteria in his book *Visible Learning for Teachers: Maximizing Impact on Learning*. In this book, Hattie shares a meta-analysis of more than 15 years of research involving thousands of students to provide evidence about what works to improve learning. He stresses that teachers and students must have a clear and shared understanding of both the learning intentions (what students are expected to learn) and success criteria (what success looks like in the end).

> The aim is to get the students actively involved in seeking this evidence: their role is not simply to do tasks as decided by teachers, but to actively manage and understand their learning gains. This includes evaluating their own progress, being more responsible for their learning, and being involved with peers in learning together about gains in learning. (p. 98)

Hattie then uses an analogy to illustrate the importance of success criteria:

> Imagine if I were simply to ask you to get in your car and drive; at some unspecified time, I will let you know when you have successfully arrived (if you arrive at all). For too many students, this is what learning feels like. (p. 56)

I like to think of learning intentions and success criteria as a teacher and student version of Pinterest. When you want to create or learn something new, you type in your search terms (learning standard), and a visual of the product appears, along with a narrative explaining the different steps (learning intentions) and the success criteria (what success at each step looks like). This is the exact thing you want to emulate in your classrooms. What are your learning intentions? What are your success criteria? Are they all aligned to the standard, allowing students to be autonomous in how they show their understanding?

Then, instead of coming up with the vehicle (product) students will use to demonstrate their learning, let students generate a list of possible ways to show their understanding. When students create the list, teachers avoid inadvertently asking students to engage in a learning activity that is not empathetic.

Figure 2.2 shows a nonacademic example of planning instruction (baking a cake), while Figure 2.3 illustrates how to redo the assignment in Kellie's story to plan for learning instead of doing.

Learning intentions should be based on the standards being assessed (learning) rather than the product that is to be "turned in" (doing). In Kellie's situation, her teacher focused on the eulogy rather than the components of learning (writing focus, organization, development, and conventions). Constructing lessons with a focus on learning gives students the autonomy to apply the skills they are learning to a product that makes sense in their world. Furthermore, it will provide you, their teacher, more insight into their unique perspectives, which will strengthen your ability to empathize with them moving forward.

FIGURE 2.2

Nonacademic Sample of Learning Intentions and Success Criteria

Priority Standard(s) Assessed: Bake and decorate a simple vanilla cake.

Learning Intentions (what we instruct and assess)	Success Criteria (what we look for when assessing)
1. Measure ingredients according to a recipe.	• Student measures tablespoons correctly. • Student measures teaspoons correctly. • Student measures cups correctly.
2. Mix ingredients according to a recipe.	• Student whisks dry ingredients together. • Student beats wet ingredients together until they are light and fluffy. • Student beats wet and dry ingredients together alternating (wet and dry) at an appropriate speed.
3. Bake the cake.	• Student bakes the cake until lightly golden on top and a toothpick comes out clean. • Student bakes the cake without burning it.
4. Decorate the cake.	• Student evenly frosts the entire cake using store-bought, prepared frosting. • Student ensures there is no cake seen or crumbs of cake mixed into the frosting. • Student uses at least one 3-D decoration to decorate their cake. • Student uses icing to share a message (e.g., *Happy Birthday*).
Options for Product Structure *(generated by students after the teacher shares the learning intentions and success criteria)*	• Birthday cake • Wedding cake • Kid's birthday cake • Valentine's Day cake • Halloween cake • Super Bowl Sunday cake

FIGURE 2.3

Kellie's Story Revisited with Learning Intentions and Success Criteria

Priority Standard(s) Assessed: CCSS.ELA-LITERACY.W.11-12.3.A: Write narratives to develop real or imagined experiences or events using effective technique, well-chosen details, and well-structured event sequences. Engage and orient the reader by setting out a problem, situation, or observation and its significance, establishing one or multiple point(s) of view, and introducing a narrator and/or characters; create a smooth progression of experiences or events.

Learning Intentions (what we instruct and assess)	Success Criteria (what we look for when assessing)
1. Establish a clear focus and structure addressing this prompt: *In a narrative manner: praise, honor, promote, or avenge a person, group of people, or organization using a structure of your choosing.*	• Student sufficiently addresses all aspects of the prompt. • Student strongly develops a focus on the attributes of a specific person.
2. Organize writing in a way that engages and maintains readers' attention.	• Student clearly establishes the narrator. • Student clearly establishes one or more distinct and consistent points of view that captivate readers (1st or 3rd person). • Student clearly introduces a character or characters in a compelling way that ensures the reader will keep reading. • Student clearly states the situation, problem, or observation (e.g., "It is my honor to accept this Nobel Peace Prize"). • Student maintains a smooth and logical progression of pertinent and appealing experiences or events. • Student uses transitions appropriately to connect the different parts of their narrative. • Student promotes a sense of intrigue, empathy, love, happiness, sadness, or growth with their writing. • Student ends the narrative with a sense of closure by reflecting on what is experienced, learned, or resolved during the course of the narrative.

(continued)

FIGURE 2.3

Kellie's Story Revisited with Learning Intentions and Success Criteria (*continued*)

Learning Intentions (what we instruct and assess)	Success Criteria (what we look for when assessing)

3. Develop characters or people and situations to evoke an emotional reaction in readers.	• Student creatively weaves two or more of the following narrative techniques to show the relationship between characters, events, and experiences.
	  – Dialogue
	  – Pacing
	  – Description
	  – Reflection
	  – Multiple plot lines
	• Student has appropriate pacing; student doesn't over-develop or under-develop any parts.
	• Student uses precise words and phrases to illustrate a clear and detailed picture of the events and setting.
	• Student uses sensory language to illustrate a vivid picture that engages readers and fully captures the characters' motivation, actions, experiences, and events.
	• Student promotes a sense of intrigue, empathy, love, happiness, sadness, or other emotion (theme) with their writing.

4. Use conventions properly.	• Student demonstrates a well-developed command of standard English conventions with few, if any, usage errors. • Student consistently uses correct punctuation, spelling, and capitalization, which contributes to the coherence of the narrative.
Options for Product Structure *(generated by students after teacher shares the learning intentions and success criteria)*	• Wedding vows or speech • Acceptance speech to receive an award • Speech to present an award to a recipient • Eulogy • Letter of apology • Letter of recommendation

Reflect: What role does empathy play in designing curriculum and instruction?

Try This: When lesson planning, focus on what students are *to learn*, not what students are *to do*. Determine the learning first, then plan the activities. Use the checklist in Figure 2.4 to design curriculum that promotes a more empathetic learning experience for your students.

FIGURE 2.4
Teacher Clarity Checklist

- ❑ Identify the focus learning standard or standards for your unit of study. Use the REAL criteria (Many & Horrell, 2014):
  - ○ **Readiness:** This standard provides students with essential knowledge and skills necessary for success in the next class, course, or grade level.
  - ○ **Endurance:** This standard provides students with knowledge and skills that are useful beyond a single test or unit of study.
  - ○ **Assessed:** This standard will be assessed on upcoming state and national exams.
  - ○ **Leverage:** This standard will provide students with the knowledge and skills that will be of value in multiple disciplines.
- ❑ Clarify the learning intentions (what students are to learn or master) for the standard.
- ❑ Determine success criteria (what constitutes mastery or proficiency of each learning intention).
- ❑ Ensure that all success criteria are aligned to the standard (i.e., if there are things that you would *like* for students to do, but are not necessary to show mastery, make these expectations, not mandates).
- ❑ Model what success looks like for students.
- ❑ Ask students to generate a list of ways (e.g., products) they can demonstrate the success criteria.

3

The Empathetic Learning
Environment

A large portion of my work as an educational consultant is partnering with school districts to build instructional coaching programs. In this role, I work side by side with instructional coaches, visiting classrooms together, attending coaching meetings with teachers together, and debriefing afterward to determine the best approaches for meeting teachers' goals.

One of the most frequent requests for support that I receive from the coaches I work with is classroom management (specifically undesirable student behaviors). Sometimes teachers struggle with an entire group of students; other times, teachers are particularly concerned about one or two students. In these cases, a specific request for support from coaches that I hear quite often is something like, *"I am working with a teacher who is struggling with a student. The teacher reports that this student goes from 0 to 10 with no warning."*

To which I always respond, "Let's set up a time to visit this classroom as soon as possible. My guess is that the student didn't go from 0 to 10 with no warning, but rather, the teacher (through no fault of his or her own) missed 1–9."

As stated at the beginning of this book, the percentage of our students who have experienced trauma is at an all-time high. In 2020, the U.S. Department of Health & Human Services reported that up to two-thirds of students have or are currently experiencing trauma (SAMHSA, 2020).

Trauma is defined at its simplest as undergoing profoundly distressing or disturbing experiences. Traumatic experiences include, but are not limited to, neglect; physical, psychological, or sexual abuse; natural disasters; unsafe or unpredictable living conditions; and witnessing violence.

Students who experience trauma are prone to engage in negative self-talk, have trouble trusting people, are on high-alert at all times, and often present with behaviors like avoidance, aggression, shutting down, outbursts, and other behaviors (Jennings & Siegel, 2019). Traumatized students have many triggers (situations that feel similar to or reenact elements of the trauma), including fear of failure, uncertainty, power struggles, sensory overload, insufficient sensory input, and more. Once triggered, trauma victims will enter flight, fight, or freeze mode, which can manifest in various ways, from violent outbursts to dissociating (separating from oneself; can appear like "zoning out").

Additionally, the number of students with an Autism Spectrum Disorder (ASD) is growing, with 1 in 54 students presenting with such (CDC, 2020). Interestingly, ASD individuals are also triggered by some of the same things as students who experienced trauma: uncertainty, sensory overload or underload, and others. Like trauma students, once triggered, ASD students react in various ways: meltdowns, outbursts, shutting down, and more. This is not to say that Autism Spectrum Disorders are a form of trauma; rather, with the increase in the number of trauma victims *and* students with ASD, the need for educators to respond with empathetic strategies like the ones outlined in this chapter is essential to student learning.

It follows, I think, that you must create learning environments with the same intention and using the same empathetic lens as when you plan instruction. To garner the highest success rate with all students, you must maximize proactivity in your measures and minimize reactivity. You accomplish this by exercising empathy with a focus on these eight guideposts:

1. Eliminating trauma triggers, not fixing traumatized students
2. Ensuring teacher clarity for classroom management
3. Cultivating a sense of belonging by building relationships
4. Promoting feelings
5. Tapping into intrinsic motivation rather than extrinsic rewards
6. Giving consequences instead of punishments
7. Having restorative conversations
8. Practicing self-care

It is important to note that while you can significantly reduce the number and intensity of occurrences, addressing the needs of traumatized students with an empathetic lens is hard work. Compassion fatigue is real, and service workers (e.g., teachers, nurses, first responders) are more vulnerable to this condition.

You must, therefore, be mindful of your own mental health and engage in self-care, which I will address in this chapter.

Focus on *Eliminating* Trauma Triggers, Not *Fixing* Traumatized Students

Let's return to the example at the beginning of this chapter—the teacher who was struggling with a student who was going from 0 to 10 with no apparent warning. Let's examine the learning environment in that classroom at the time. The coach and I scheduled a time to visit the teacher's class (a 3rd grade art section). Before our visit, I asked the coach to identify examples of "10" behaviors. The coach reported that the teacher described a student who was saying inappropriate things to her and other students. When she asked him to stop, he would become loud, defiant, and uncontrollable; she usually had to call someone to remove him from the classroom.

I asked the coach not to tell me who the student of concern was. I wanted to observe the classroom as a whole (i.e., teacher, other students, environment) and see if I saw any possible "triggers" that may result in undesirable student behavior. I did this because teachers often *see* the student who responds with the loudest, most prominent, most apparent response, then they try to *fix* that student. Meanwhile, the triggers that set off the most adverse student reactions are likely affecting other students similarly. Those students might respond in less noticeable ways or completely internalize their reactions, but their learning may also be compromised. Therefore, teachers need to look at eliminating the triggers rather than reacting with punishments or consequences. I asked the coach to do the same while focusing on the student of concern because the coach knew who this student was.

The coach and I walked into a classroom that was well-maintained and inviting. The 18 students were sitting in pods of three or four. The bell rang, and the teacher began class—and the first thing I noticed was the teacher using a microphone. I noted this as possible trigger #1.

Next, the teacher said, "We are going to continue working on our perspective landscapes that we started last week." I noted this as possible trigger #2.

Then, the teacher said, "Please go get your materials." I noted this as possible trigger #3.

At this point, about half of the students got up and went to source materials. The other students stayed in their seats or stood up and watched what their classmates were getting. A few students started talking or rocking in their chairs.

At this point, the teacher said, "I should see everybody out of their seats getting their materials." I noted this as possible trigger #4.

A few more students got up; a couple asked their peers what they should be getting, and a couple just wandered around the room. Many still did not make any effort to get their materials. Now, the teacher said, "I'm not sure why so many of you aren't getting your things, especially after I've asked you several times. Can someone who is following directions please tell your classmates what they should be doing?" I noted this as possible trigger #5.

This had all occurred within the first five minutes of class. The students had not begun their learning yet.

At this point, I also noted that one of the boys who was not getting up started writing on his tablemate's paper and reciting provocative lines from the movie *Uncle Buck*. None of the students at his pod seemed to mind at all. I now had a pretty good idea of who the student of concern was. This student was not causing a scene, yet, but he was undoubtedly displaying indicators that he was becoming "unhinged"—the missing 1–9.

As the learning progressed, I could see the student of interest becoming agitated (part of the missing 1–9), but his behaviors were subtle and unknown to the teacher.

Now, you may be wondering why I noted the five items that I did. So, let's think about these items through the lens of empathy. (See Figure 3.1 for examples of potential triggers from this classroom example and reasons they are triggering.) Are you feeling with your students? Do you see things from their perspective? Are you acting to empathize, or are you dismissing student perspective and potentially causing more damage?

Ensure Teacher Clarity for Classroom Management

Thinking back to some of the commonly seen behaviors in trauma victims—shutting down, increased aggression, defiance—you can see how the triggers from the previous section could seem inconsequential in isolation but cumulatively could result in a "10" reaction.

Human behaviors are all motivated by one or more of four functions:

1. To escape or avoid something
2. To get attention
3. To gain something tangible
4. To receive or eliminate sensory input (e.g., taste, smell, touch, visual)

FIGURE 3.1

Viewing Triggers with an Empathy Lens

Potential Trigger	Why?
Teacher use of microphone	• The sensory input was too great (especially for ASD students). • The power dynamic created may be off-putting and may lead to retraumatization in traumatized students (Jennings & Siegel, 2019).
"We are going to continue working on our perspective landscapes that we started last week."	• Students may not have been in class last week or, if they were, might not recall what the perspective landscape is or what the learning intentions or success criteria are. • Uncertainty causes anxiety, fear of failure, or shame for all students, with a significantly higher likelihood of triggering traumatized and ASD students.
"Please go get your materials."	• This statement is unclear. Which materials exactly? Where do you get them? Again, uncertainty causes anxiety, fear of failure, or shame for all students, with a significantly higher likelihood of triggering traumatized and ASD students.
"I should see everybody out of their seats getting their materials."	• This statement could shame students who still don't know what materials they should be getting or even what they are learning or practicing.
"I'm not sure why there are so many of you who aren't getting your things, especially after I've asked you several times. Can someone who is following directions please tell your classmates what they should be doing?"	• This statement exacerbates the divide between "good students" and "bad students." This can confirm the negative internal dialogue students have with themselves resulted in increased undesirable behavior, sometimes known as a self-fulfilling prophecy.

All humans respond with these behaviors. It becomes problematic when the actions are unsafe, stigmatize, or interfere with learning. For many students, however, any response is better than no response, so undesirable behaviors are inadvertently reinforced when not appropriately addressed (Minahan & Rappaport, 2013, p. 16).

Once again, this process starts with **teacher clarity.** In this case, we need clarity of expectations for learning, behaving, seeking help when needed, and so on.

So, how are the situations from this example remedied? The short answer is through questioning and reflection. As an instructional coach, I partner with teachers to help induce reflection. I don't assume I know the answers or give directives. I ask a lot of questions to help my coachees set goals and then offer choices as to how to meet those goals. These questions help teachers critically assess their practices in a safe environment to determine what works best and what does not. Even if you do not have an instructional coach, you can apply this same practice and question yourself to reflect. The bonus is that questioning as a practice also works with students of all ages and, if done properly, is highly empathetic.

Take, for example, the first trigger: the microphone. Rather than telling the teacher that the microphone may be causing students sensory distress or inadvertently creating a power dynamic, we start with questions. We begin with empathy. We focus on strengths.

> **Coach:** Thank you so much for inviting me into your classroom today; it helped me see you in action with your students. I was also super-impressed with the 3rd graders' perspective drawing skills!
>
> **Teacher:** Thank you! I'm pleased with that, too. I just wish I could get to all of my students. I'm really interested to hear your thoughts on this.
>
> **Coach:** I understand how you feel. It's hard to focus on all of your successes when even one student is struggling.
>
> **Teacher:** Yes, exactly!
>
> **Coach:** So, let's get started. I have a few questions for you, if that's OK.
>
> **Teacher:** Sure!
>
> **Coach:** I noticed you were using a microphone to instruct. Is that standard protocol in this building?
>
> **Teacher:** No.
>
> **Coach:** OK. Have you always used a microphone?
>
> **Teacher:** No, I started using one about a month ago.
>
> **Coach:** Ah, can you tell me why you opted for the microphone?
>
> **Teacher:** Yes. My students weren't listening to me; it was challenging to start class and even more challenging to keep their attention. So, I got the microphone so that they could hear me better.
>
> **Coach:** Oh, I see. And is that working for you?
>
> **Teacher:** Not really. I mean, they settle down quicker, but they still don't follow directions.

Through this questioning, we got to the real root of what is likely to have the most positive effect on students: teacher clarity. I wanted to focus on this with the teacher because so many times, students will "act out" when things are unclear to them.

Looking at the four motivations for student behavior—to escape or avoid something, to get attention, to gain something tangible, or to receive or eliminate sensory input—this actually makes a lot of sense. We know that shame often results when students' needs are not met with empathetic responses, and students will frequently do anything to avoid the intense, negative feelings of shame, even if some of those behaviors appear to be counterproductive. Trauma victims in particular often carry a massive load of shame with them at all times and are threatened by the notion of additional shame. As a result, their behaviors are often to avoid shame—the shame of not knowing what materials to get or how to perform a task. Shouting out or shutting down is their flight or fight response to avoid looking like they are "less than." It is easier to present as "I don't want to do this dumb project" than admit they don't know what they are supposed to be doing or don't have the skills necessary to engage in the learning task at hand. Once again, therefore, we start with clarity: identify systems and structures to provide clarity for students, or better yet, involve students in the process.

For instance, using our art example:

> Good morning, boys and girls. Today we are continuing to use size relationship and overlapping to create the element of depth. Take a look at my example here using fence posts and balls. Now take a look at your success criteria checklist. Turn and talk to your shoulder partner. Partner A share one example of how size is being used in this example. Partner B, please write this down. You will have three minutes for this task. I will raise my hand at the end of three minutes. When you see my hand up, please raise your hand, too, and end your conversations.

Notice how there was clarity in the task as well as the academics. Having A and B partners allows the teacher to control which student does what. A student who has lower shame resilience would be Student B, the scribe. Student A likely has higher shame resilience and so would be better equipped to take on the more intimidating task of sharing thoughts. Regardless, in the end, both students are engaging with the task at hand, and that helps them internalize the expectations with tangible examples.

When it comes time to gather materials, structure also proves helpful. Here are just two ideas:

1. Post a short list (with visuals if possible) of materials to gather and have students reference the list.

2. In small groups, ask students to generate the list of materials they will need to complete their work. Review the lists and prompt students to add or delete any items through questioning; *"I see you have markers on your list. Can you tell me what you plan to do with markers?"* Perhaps you had colored pencils in mind, but markers may suffice. The questioning, rather than the telling, demonstrates the perspective level of empathy. After agreeing on a list of items, ask students, "Do you know where to find all of these items?" After ensuring understanding, prompt students to gather the identified materials. This process helps ensure clarity about not only what materials are needed but also why.

With the addition of a consistent attention signal (hand raising in this instance) and clarity around the academics and process of learning, a microphone should no longer be necessary. The teacher is not fighting to get or keep her students' attention. She is meeting them where they are and patiently waiting for students to come back together. With mutual respect, this will happen quite smoothly.

 Try This: Create an attention signal. Consider a signal that isn't jarring (like clapping might be) that allows all students to transition between activities safely.

Cultivate a Sense of Belonging by Building Relationships

A sense of belonging is a "fundamental human motive," says clinical psychologist Paul Rasmussen in *The Quest to Feel Good* (2010, p. 43). Feeling like one belongs to a group is directly correlated to self-esteem. Considering all of the trials and tribulations of growing up, figuring out who one is and isn't, the idea of belonging can seem foreign to all students, especially to those students who identify with an "othered group." Belonging to a learning community, therefore, should be built on the shared experience of learning, not race, religion, gender, weight, socioeconomic status, test scores, and so on. We are all part of this community that centers around learning and growing both academically and socially and emotionally.

Trauma can be cyclical (often called intergenerational trauma) and self-perpetuating (a parent raised by an alcoholic parent falling ill to alcoholism himself and exposing his child to the same trauma). But many times, the opposite happens, and people who experience trauma become even more empathetic and often help others through their trauma (often called altruism born of suffering). Researchers don't definitively know what causes some to become more empathetic and others to perpetuate (often unknowingly) trauma, but they have identified that one crucial factor: belonging. If, after a trauma, individuals feel a sense of belonging to a community, they are more likely to recover from their trauma (Zaki, 2019).

To start, you must focus on building mutually respectful relationships between you and your students. Russell Quaglia, Michael Corso, and their team at the Quaglia Institute for Student Aspirations collect and analyze data on how different stakeholder groups feel about their educational experiences. The Quaglia Institute's 2016 *National School Voice Report* disclosed a statistic that is, simply put, shocking. After surveying over 48,000 students in grades 6–12, the researchers found that only 58 percent of students felt like their teachers respected them, while 99 percent of teachers reported that they respected their students (Quaglia Institute for School Voice and Aspirations, 2016).

The discrepancy between these numbers is alarming but not surprising. It is primarily because of how we define respect between teachers and students and the steps we take to develop respectful relationships with them. In my first book, *Student-Driven Differentiation*, I describe three tenets of forming mutually respectful teacher–student relationships as informed by Quaglia and Corso's research (Westman, 2018).

Tenet 1: Be Real

Have you ever run into a student outside of school? Perhaps you bumped into a student and his mom as you turned the corner at the grocery store. Or, worse, you look up from slathering sunscreen on yourself or your children at the public pool to see your former student peeking at you from behind the water slide.

If you have, you may have felt uncomfortable when you made eye contact with your student, and you may have sensed that your level of uncomfortableness was nothing compared to theirs. It's as if students are shocked when they realize that *teachers have real lives, too.*

You must, therefore, be intentional about showing students that you are "real" and experience the same things that they do. Contrary to what logic tells us, one of the best times to find common ground is when students are off task.

Think about the student described at the beginning of this chapter, for example. One of this student's off-task behaviors was talking about the movie *Uncle Buck*. In fact, that off-task behavior was an opportunity to find common ground. Instead of reprimanding the student or shaming him for reciting provocative lines from the film, you could say something like, "Oh my gosh, *Uncle Buck*! That's a movie from my generation. I love that you've seen that movie. Interestingly, I have an uncle who we call Uncle Buck because of his inappropriate language, so I totally get you on that." Then redirect with, "Oh my gosh, I'm so sorry I just distracted you all from your learning. I'll let you get back on track now. Do you need help figuring out what to do next?"

Being real with students is also crucial when students experience a profound change in their lives (e.g., death in the family, divorce, eviction) or a chronic struggle (e.g., learning difference, negative feeling toward self).

In these situations, teachers often feel the need to make things right for these students or, conversely, pretend like the problem doesn't exist so that the student doesn't get upset. But we must resist these urges and just respond by being real—that is, with empathy.

> This is probably a confusing time for you now. I am so sorry you have been experiencing this. I can't understand [unless you have had the same situation] your exact circumstances, so I won't pretend to imagine I know exactly what you are feeling. But I have experienced loss [or fear or whatever emotion], and it was helpful for me to know other people understood that I was experiencing a range of emotions and didn't judge me for that. I'd do the same for you.

Tenet 2: Be Consistent

Humans thrive on consistency. Knowing what to expect and when is hugely comforting, especially to trauma victims and those on the autism spectrum.

But because we are only human, we tend to respond inconsistently to similar situations, depending on who is involved. We may exhibit the utmost patience with our students if they misplace something but fly off the handle with our own children if they can't find their backpacks.

This sometimes happens with how we respond to "compliant" versus "defiant" students in our classrooms. We often let compliant students off the hook when they digress because they are typically "good" and then respond more quickly with harsher consequences to defiant students because they are continually breaking the rules. Sadly, inconsistent responses damage relationships with all students, contributing to self-fulfilling prophecies. The "bad" kids keep up their image, while the "good" kids are less likely to take risks because they are afraid to lose their status. For authentic, mutually respectful relationships to exist, we must be mindful of responding to situations, not individuals.

Tenet 3: Be a Listener

This is perhaps the most demanding quality to consistently demonstrate because our natural inclination is not to listen but *respond*. Sprinkled throughout this book are examples that show the best way to listen is to ask more questions and make fewer statements. When you are listening, try to do so without judgment in an effort to see things from the student's perspective. My daughter recently shared an interaction with her teacher where she asked why they had a test on the same day as standardized testing. The teacher responded, "Because that's when we are having it." I can certainly see why the teacher might feel defensive. But rather than respond with a dismissive statement, the teacher could have asked why my daughter wanted to know. This would have elicited context about my daughter's fear of testing fatigue affecting her grade and allowed the teacher to both empathize and strengthen her relationship with my daughter.

> **Try This:** Create a list of three nonnegotiable behaviors that you expect students to practice. Then, determine how you will respond to students (regardless of who they are) when they do not exhibit a behavior the first time, the second time, and the third time. Keep this checklist on hand (e.g., on your desk, on your iPad) and consult it before responding or reacting to ensure your responses are consistent. **Bonus:** Make sure one step includes asking students a question to gain insight into their perspectives.

Promote Feelings

When I read Mark Brackett's *Permission to Feel*, I learned that when it comes to identifying how we feel, we, for a variety of reasons, often misidentify our feelings or don't admit how we truly feel.

Considering that empathy begins with identifying with another's feelings, recognizing our own emotions is crucial. It is also imperative that teachers help students identify their feelings and, more important, that they validate students' feelings, rather than admonish them for feeling a certain way.

You can do this in your classrooms in a variety of ways. The first is to *practice*. As the director of the Yale Center for Emotional Intelligence, Brackett and his team created the Mood Meter app (www.moodmeterapp.com), a tool that helps users build their emotional vocabulary (bonus for writing and reading, too). It guides users to accurately identify how they feel, provides healthy redirection options, and tracks feelings by day and time to identify trends. This free app is one great way to practice identifying your own feelings and helping your students to do the same. I recommend using it or others like it in your classroom.

Second, you can *allow students to feel*. Teachers often (with positive yet misguided intentions) condemn students for their feelings instead of allowing them to experience their emotions and redirect their actions that result from certain behaviors. For example, if a student gets angry and throws something, you tell them to control their anger. You might create elaborate tracking systems that allow students to earn points if they make it all day without getting angry. But if a student feels angry, you should be asking why. Tell them it's OK to feel angry but not to throw things. Ask them what else they can do when they feel mad that's not going to hurt them or someone else. The Mood Meter app and the template illustrated in Figure 3.2 can help with this. Because the writing option is off-putting for some students, be sure to give them alternatives, like using the template in a digital format or audio or video recording their responses. The goal is for students to reflect, not for students to complete a worksheet.

To have students earn points for not having an outburst (when this outburst is the result of feeling angry), you are implicitly telling this child that feeling angry is undesired, in essence, shaming this child for how they think and feel.

To add fuel to the fire, teachers often reward students for repressing feelings with extrinsic rewards like candy bars or banking minutes of a video game. In essence, they are telling students to suppress their emotion and they will be rewarded with sugar or video games, two highly addictive substances. This inadvertently teaches students to self-soothe with addictive properties, which perhaps explains the astounding fact that 70 percent of substance abusers experienced trauma as children (Khoury, Tang, Bradley, Cubells, & Ressler, 2010).

Instead, you can encourage students to feel. Validate their feelings. Then, help them find appropriate ways to respond to those feelings if needed. And, in a true empathetic manner, students need to be part of this process. You may be able to identify a strategy that works to de-escalate your own anger, but that strategy may not work for students. Therefore, you can offer suggestions, ask students if they have ideas, and try various things until you find something that works.

Be careful of one-size-fits-all approaches. Instead, offer options that vary in sensory input. Some people respond to cooling off alone in a reflection room, while others are better off redirecting themselves in the company of others because being alone is also triggering.

Try This: Have students track their feelings and effective strategies for coping with their feelings using a chart like the examples in Figures 3.2 and 3.3.

FIGURE 3.2

Identifying and Redirecting Feelings, Part 1

What Is Happening? (circle one)	How Do You Feel? (circle one)	Need a Calming Strategy? (circle one)
(icons)	(emoji icons)	(icons)
	Draw your own:	Other:

FIGURE 3.3

Identifying and Redirecting Feelings, Part 2

How Do You Feel? *Circle one.*	Can You Identify Why? *What is happening right now? Where are you? Who is with you? Did something happen before school today?*	Is a Calming Strategy Needed? *If so, choose a strategy to help you process how you feel.*	Was This Strategy Effective? *Why or why not?*
Happy		Play with a fidget toy.	
Sad		Walk down the hallway and back.	
Angry		Visit the reflection room.	
Scared		Bounce on a yoga ball.	
Nervous		Read a book.	
Disappointed		Look at photographs.	
Frustrated		Draw a picture.	
Bored		Write in your journal.	
Other:		Other:	

Tap into Intrinsic Motivation Rather Than Extrinsic Rewards

Earlier in this chapter, I addressed the idea of rewarding students with tangible objects for exhibiting desired behaviors and emotions and pointed out the critical flaws in these practices. In general, the cumulative effect of using extrinsic motivators (e.g., parties, treats, money, grades) is to decrease motivation and desire. We are all born intrinsically motivated (no one offers us a $100 or an A to learn to walk). Reverting to intrinsic motivation foundations—purpose, autonomy, and mastery—will always result in a higher yield. But because our world is so heavily focused on extrinsic rewards, this will take time. It's worth keeping in mind, however, and perhaps something worth trying in your classroom or school.

Read and Reflect

Read this vignette from Stefanie Rothstein, an SEL coordinator and cofounder of Learning Minnesota, as she reflects on intrinsic versus extrinsic motivation. What resonates with you about her perspective? What piques your interest?

Intrinsic Versus Extrinsic Motivation

By Stefanie Rothstein

"Thanks for opening the door for me! Here's a B.U.G. Buck."
"Wow! You were really quiet in the hall today. Let's add a marble to the class jar."
"Congratulations on having the entire class get their calculus assignments in on time last week! For that, we're showering you with Smarties!"

These are just a few of the many phrases I've experienced in my 15 years working in education. As much as I believe in the power of positive interactions and experiences, I am saddened that what should be considered normal human behavior (opening doors, respecting others' learning, meeting deadlines) has become something kids are rewarded for doing.

Picture this: You're moving to enter your building and see a colleague approaching to enter as well. You open the door and stand for a moment longer to hold the door for your colleague. After both of you have entered the building, the assistant principal exclaims that she is proud of you for holding the door open and proceeds to hand you a slip of paper you can use to enter into a drawing for a marker, sticker, or donated fast-food toy at the end of the week.

Or this: You're on lunch and remember you have to make copies quickly before picking up your class. You proceed to the copy room to make your copies and are caught by your principal, who announces that he is impressed at your ability to be quiet in the hall for others who are teaching. He then shares that he's going to add your name to the staff marble jar that, when full, initiates a staff party.

Do either of these scenarios strike you as odd? Or even a bit insulting? If so, take a moment to reflect on why it doesn't seem so when we do it for students.

By actively rewarding kids with tangibles or quick, inauthentic words of praise, we compromise their innate ability to develop a social-emotional repertoire as human beings. Instead of reflecting on the impact their actions have on others by observing others' reactions, we are conditioning children in the same way television shows condition the brain to expect entertainment. The longer school systems and classrooms spend time on initiatives that offer extrinsic rewards for positive behaviors and actions, the greater the effort necessary to ensure students unlearn this falsity.

As educators, we commit to serving the students whose families entrust us with their care and guidance and intentionally mold and shape what we envision the future of our world to be. By providing students with the opportunity to recognize the natural, intrinsic motivators that accompany positive behaviors, we shape a future that includes a greater ability to think, collaborate, have authentic conversations, and create critically.

By empowering our students to be drivers of their learning journeys, we are amplifying their internal motivators. And how do we, as educators, undertake such a significant shift in approach and planning? By taking those small moments to wipe potential smears from our lenses so that we can more clearly see each and every one of the humans we serve. Through intentional empathetic approaches, we deliver to our students learning experiences that promote their individual needs of freedom and flexibility. All that is left is to toss them the keys.

Give Consequences Instead of Punishments

Although applying the strategies and suggestions from this chapter to create empathetic learning communities will certainly result in more harmonious learning environments, they will not eliminate the need for redirection. Empathy is commonly mistaken for "going easy" on someone because we understand their "why," but this is an oversimplification. We may understand why a student acts in a certain way, but that does not mean that their actions are acceptable. Part of empathizing as an educator (or a parent) is to empathize with feelings and perspectives while also setting clear expectations and boundaries and redirecting students when necessary (Riess, 2018, p. 88).

I've spent quite a bit of time talking about the damage shame causes to our self-image and our ability to self-regulate and about the profound barrier shame creates around empathy. Choosing how to redirect behavior is no different; shame is also catastrophic, and shaming a student will not lead to changed behavior (Brown, 2007, p. 62).

There is a difference, however, between shame and guilt. Shame is about people, their identities, and traits; guilt is about actions. A person can feel guilt for something and not be shamed for that. In fact, guilt is a healthy indicator of being empathetic. If you feel guilty about your actions, you recognize how your actions affect other people.

It is OK for children to feel guilty for an action they intentionally or inadvertently committed; it is not OK for you to shame them for it. This is where you must look to restorative practices (i.e., consequences) over punishment (i.e., shaming mechanisms).

Consequences differ from punishments in that they again center around the action, not the person. There are two types of consequences: natural consequences and logical consequences (Anderson, 2018).

Natural consequences are the effects that organically occur from an action that helps us regulate our behavior. For instance, if a student oversleeps and misses the bus, a natural consequence is that he had to walk two miles to school. This consequence would likely be effective in changing the student's action (remembering to set an alarm). Conversely, suppose a student is late to school because his parents overslept (something beyond the student's control and perhaps a symptom of more significant trauma at home). In that case, the punishment of a detention after school is unlikely to result in changed behavior. Furthermore, the punishment shames the student for who they are (a kid with an unreliable parent) rather than their personal actions, which lead to healthy guilt.

Logical consequences are given to students by an adult. They address the specific behavior or action, are respectful of the student, and are reasonable (Anderson, 2018). A logical consequence for a student who is late to school would be to have that student meet with his teacher or a designated peer to find out what he missed in the classes he missed, then provide the student with an option of making up that learning or time by, for example, staying for homework help, reading notes, or watching a video.

One example of a common classroom practice that highlights the importance of empathy and consequences versus punishments is the use of clip-up/clip-down classroom behavior charts. I'm often asked if these tools, which allow a teacher to track students' behavior throughout a day, are OK. I always answer, "It depends. Are the charts you are using effective in identifying specific behaviors, respectfully, and do they offer reasonable options to correct behavior?" In most instances, the answer to this question is "no," which leaves me strongly inclined to recommend discontinuing their use because, without these criteria, the charts mainly identify "good" and "bad" students for who they are rather than for their actions. In general, clip charts are thoroughly unempathetic and run a significant risk of shaming students. They typically work well for students who make an occasional transgression but are especially ineffective for students who are regular transgressors.

After working with hundreds of teachers who use clip charts and feel unarmed to address behaviors without them, I also recognize that it's not as easy as just throwing the charts away. If you fall into this category, then I suggest going slowly. Start your school year with a chart. As soon as you have a student get three "reds," use that data to tell you that the chart is ineffective in changing that student's behavior and differentiate your approach for that student. Instead of the clip chart, try using some of the other strategies in this chapter, like tracking emotions, choosing calming techniques, and giving logical and natural consequences.

No matter what type of consequence you deem appropriate for the student, it is crucial that the student fully understands what the transgression was, why it is not acceptable, and the purpose of the consequence. Dialogue is important and should center around questions that check for the student's understanding rather than statements sharing the teacher's account. Using questioning to ensure a mutual understanding will help preserve the student–teacher relationship.

Have Restorative Conversations

As hard as you try to be empathetic in planning and facilitating learning in your classrooms, you will have days where your efforts fall short, which can be disheartening. This is where restorative conversations are quite valuable. A restorative conversation requires both parties to own their part in a situation and share how they feel. These may be a little uncomfortable at first (especially if you or a student has low shame resilience and admitting fault is difficult). But, with practice, they get more comfortable and quite productive. Sometimes it can be a struggle to determine your part in a conflict. When this happens, you can typically own *how* you communicated. For example, you can say, "I'm sorry the way I shared that information with you made you so uncomfortable. That wasn't my intention at all."

Kellie's Story Revisited

Remember Kellie from Chapter 2, the student who received a *C-* on her English paper? Well, Kellie's story has a happy ending. After I shared her story with the workshop participants, and we reflected on the experience as a group, Kellie asked to share her story's conclusion.

She said that about 12 years after receiving a *C-* on her eulogy assignment, Kellie's mom got a call from Kellie's 12th grade English teacher. The teacher said she had recently lost her mother, and through her grieving, she kept thinking about Kellie. She asked for Kellie's phone number and called her to apologize. She shared that when she assigned that eulogy, she had never lost anyone before. She told Kellie that she vividly remembered how upset Kellie was with her grade, but it wasn't until she delivered the eulogy at her own mother's funeral that she understood what a personal experience it was. Then the teacher said, "I'm sorry for assigning that piece. Moreover, when you asked me about it, I'm sorry I didn't have the insight and courage to hear your perspective."

This, I explained to the group, was a perfect example of "owning your part."

In the two years since Kellie first shared this story with me, I have told it at dozens of workshops. This story typically initiates a rich discussion among participants. But, one time, something even more remarkable happened. One participant called me over and said, "This is my 23rd year teaching in this district. You see that teacher on the other side of the room with the blond hair and striped shirt? I taught her when she was in 8th grade, and about five years ago, she started working here. And I've been avoiding her ever since."

When I asked why, the teacher explained, "One time she fell asleep in my class. And to wake her up, I slammed on the bottom of her desk. She woke up, was startled, and the other students started laughing. I shouldn't have done that. I'm worried that I shamed her."

I asked her if she would be willing to talk to the younger teacher about it. She agreed, and I asked the former student, now teacher, Michelle (a pseud-onym), to join us at the veteran teacher's table, where they had the following conversation:

> **Veteran teacher:** Hi, Michelle, I don't know if you remember me, but I was your teacher in 8th grade.
>
> **Michelle:** Hi, I remember you.
>
> **Veteran teacher:** I wanted to apologize to you. You fell asleep in my class once, and I slammed on your desk to wake you up. It startled you, and I should have handled that situation differently. I'm sorry.
>
> **Michelle:** Thank you for sharing this with me. I honestly don't remember this situation, but regardless, I'm sorry I fell asleep in your class. That was disrespectful and inconsiderate.

This is a perfect example of a restorative conversation in which both parties own their part and demonstrate empathy for the other person's perspective. It also exemplifies the power of empathy. Even years later, it is possible to empathize with someone even if you didn't at the time. We are always continually learning and growing and gaining new information. It is never too late to restore or to do better next time. And, as Kellie's story proves, vulnerability is contagious. Just one person who is willing to be vulnerable and share can open the doors for others to do the same.

Reflect: Think of someone (professionally or personally) whose perspective on a situation or experience is different from yours. How has this affected your relationship? What part of this situation can you own?

Try This: Would you like to improve or restore your relationship? Consider sharing your reflections with this person. This is not to induce their ownership in the situation (we cannot control other people). It is merely to practice exhibiting empathy and vulnerability.

Practice Self-Care

Similar to how air travel safety regulations require you to secure your oxygen mask before assisting others with theirs, you must first take care of your own mental health needs. You must embody empathy by empathizing with yourself—identify your feelings, recognize your triggers, and choose healthy coping strategies—before you can model and instruct students with this process.

In *Permission to Feel,* Brackett cites that the majority of teachers in America are experiencing unpleasant feelings—regularly spending "nearly 70 percent of their workdays feeling 'frustrated,' 'overwhelmed,' and 'stressed'" (2019, p. 15).

Fortuitously, the same strategies that work for children also work for adults. You just may have to dig a little deeper to connect with yourself and allow yourself to experience whatever it is that you feel *without shaming yourself.* This is super-uncomfortable, I know. It doesn't happen overnight, but little by little, you will grow in this area. And I promise you, as soon as you become more compassionate with yourself (for your genuine emotions, the real triggers), compassion for your students and others in your life will naturally emerge.

 Try This: Commit to one of the self-care options outlined in Figure 3.4. Engage in this option until you do so without guilt, and it becomes a regular part of your routine. Then, add another!

FIGURE 3.4
Practice Self-Care

- **Get a good night's sleep:** Stick to a regular bedtime that will allow you a minimum of seven hours of sleep each night.

- **Get fresh air:** Take a daily stroll outside for a minimum of 10 minutes, rain or shine.

- **Exercise 15 minutes a day:** Whether it's yoga, cycling, walking, running, swimming, it doesn't matter. Do whatever works for you.

- **Indulge:** Treat yourself to something each month that you don't normally enjoy: a massage, a manicure, dinner at a new restaurant, a movie.

- **Socialize:** Call or visit with a friend (not text or email) to listen to the sound of their voice. Share something with them that you are feeling. Ask them to share.

- **Take up a new hobby:** Try baking, cooking, fishing, photography—something that interests *you.*

- **Feed your heart and mind:** Eat things that promote health and also satisfy you. Choose items with high fiber, protein, healthy fats. Don't deprive yourself of anything. Aim for balance.

- **Be mindful:** Get in touch with yourself and your surroundings and journal or sit with your thoughts as you take a breath and ask yourself, "What's happening around me right now? How do I feel? What input is each of my senses giving me?"

Recommended Readings

For additional reading on trauma-informed instruction and creating empathetic learning environments, I recommend the following books:

Frey, N., Fisher, D., & Smith, D. (2019). *All learning is social and emotional: Helping students develop essential skills for the classroom and beyond.* Alexandria, VA: ASCD.

Jennings, P. A., & Siegel, D. J. (2019). *The trauma-sensitive classroom: Building resilience with compassionate teaching.* New York: W.W. Norton.

Minahan, J., & Rappaport, N. (2013). *The behavior code: A practical guide to understanding and teaching the most challenging students.* Cambridge, MA: Harvard Education Press.

4

Empathy and Equity

Equity is a hotbed topic in both education and society. School districts are working ardently to instill equity in their learning communities. A growing number of school districts have created new positions like "Director of Equity" to oversee such initiatives and provide stakeholder groups with equity learning opportunities like book studies.

These efforts will certainly help enlighten us to the different histories, ongoing struggles, and needs of many commonly marginalized groups of people. Still, I often worry about the generalization of "equity." For example, if an organization engages in a book study of Robin DiAngelo's *White Fragility: Why It's So Hard for White People to Talk About Racism* (2018) (explicitly focused on equity for black people), will readers apply the same learning to other commonly marginalized groups? Perhaps. I believe, however, a more universal and practical approach to equity is to simplify the goal. The Intercultural Development Research Association (IDRA, 2020) identifies six goals of educational equity:

1. Comparably high academic achievement and other student outcomes
2. Equitable access and inclusion
3. Equitable treatment
4. Equitable opportunity to learn
5. Equitable resources
6. Accountability

These six targets can seem like a lot for teachers and administrators, especially on top of other district initiatives and mandates. For implementation purposes, educators need one overarching skill to ensure the six equity goals are met, and that, of course, is empathy.

We start and end with empathy. *When we genuinely empathize, equity is the natural result.* It is impossible to be truly empathetic and not take actions that result in more equitable outcomes. As a reminder, Chapter 1 introduced the three types of empathy:

- **Affective:** feeling the feelings of others
- **Cognitive:** feeling from the perspective of others (all others, not just people who are similar to us)
- **Behavioral:** taking action

Behavioral empathy, as the "call to action" that results after we practice affective and cognitive empathy, will organically result in equity practices aligned with the six goals set out by the IDRA. When we feel with others from their perspective, we are compelled to take actions. Those actions result in more equitable practices because it is simply not empathetic to continue inequitable practices. Because behavioral empathy is a function of both affective and cognitive empathy, we must strengthen all three types to ensure our schools are equitable learning environments.

In this chapter, I will highlight how you can harness the power of empathy to actualize equity in your school systems.

See People as Individuals First

As illustrated in Chapter 1, we naturally tend to empathize more with people like ourselves, and we tend to "other" groups of people who are different from us.

In the United States, we divide students into subgroups (e.g., free- and reduced-price lunch, black, Asian, Native American, IEP, English learners). If you are white and do not fall into another subgroup, it is likely that you unconsciously "other" many of these subgroups on some level. Furthermore, you are implicitly comparing subgroups to a white, moderately affluent "norm." This system, in and of itself, is not empathetic.

Fixing the system is beyond the scope of this book, but you can control how you see students on a day-to-day basis. If you focus on students as individuals and demonstrate behavioral empathetic practices like those described here, you will see individual students grow and collectively close achievement gaps.

Flip the Script: Focus on Strengths, Not Deficits

The deficit model of education has worn us all down. In U.S. schools, we are hyperfocused on the deficits (or the kinder term, "areas for growth") of students, teachers, and administrators. We spend so much time beating ourselves up about the areas where data show we need improvement that we forget about our strengths. And no one is pointing them out to us.

Our expectations are flawed. In theory, we expect all students to master all standards; all teachers to be proficient at numerous criteria in various categories; and all administrators to cross every *t* and dot every *i*, always. This notion is severely lacking in empathy, in seeing people as individuals with areas of strength and areas for development. Rather, it minimizes empathy by shaming students for their deficits rather than celebrating them for their strengths.

How so? Think about this. When a student, teacher, or administrator demonstrates expertise in one area (*a student is strong in reading, a teacher is strong in curriculum mapping, an administrator has strong parent communication*), we give them a quick pat on the back and then immediately present them with their deficit (*the student needs to work on math computation, the teacher needs to differentiate, the administrator needs to improve student test scores*). We don't celebrate someone's strength and recognize how this strength could be, and likely is, something the person feels proud of. We don't ask ourselves how we can capitalize that strength. And we don't ask questions to gain perspective. Instead, we focus on the areas that aren't strengths—ultimately, frequently, leaving the person feeling defeated.

What if, instead of focusing on what students can't do, teachers won't do, or administrators didn't do, we use a more empathetic lens and focus on what we can all accomplish together? How might education look different?

To do this, we must adopt systems that authentically detect individual's specific strengths, share these strengths publicly, and create a culture where we tap into one another's strengths to build capacity, ultimately benefiting our organizations and the field of education on the whole. We need to retrain our minds to start looking for the skills and qualities that set people apart and focus solely on that.

One idea that can work if properly implemented is something I refer to as a reverse pineapple chart. The traditional pineapple chart is a popular professional learning system that allows teachers to invite one another into their classrooms for informal observation (Gonzalez, 2016). The chart is set up in a common location: the teacher's lounge, the copy room, a hallway, for example.

I propose that rather than putting the onus on yourself to promote your own strengths, you create a reverse pineapple chart (see Figure 4.1 for an example) to promote one another's strengths and start by sharing these observations.

FIGURE 4.1
Reverse Pineapple Chart

Carmen	Rich	Yael
Does making parent phone calls make you nervous? Me, too! I noticed that Carmen is always able to communicate sensitive information to parents in a clear, calm, and caring manner. She modeled a couple of parent phone calls for me and then coached me through a difficult parent situation. Crisis averted! Thank you, Carmen!	I was in Rich's classroom the other day and his passion for his content area (art) is contagious! I would love to be a student in his class on a daily basis!	Yael's approach to goal setting with her students is awesome! She has the ability to really listen to what her students say, recap their thoughts, and guide them to create meaningful goals connected to the learning target.

When the culture of sharing builds, you can hang the chart in a high-traffic area in the school. The items you celebrate must be authentic and unique, not general statements like, "John is child centered." The key is that everyone is looking at one another to find the good and recognize them for these strengths.

You can use the same process with students in your classroom or with administrators in the central offices. I encourage you to begin this process by focusing on adults' strengths, modeling compassion and positivity, and letting that process naturally trickle down to students. By using strategies that promote strengths over needs, you can create school climates where applause drowns out protest (Westman, 2017b).

Try This: 1. Partner with a trusted colleague and observe each other teaching. Identify a strength about your colleague's teaching and have your colleague do the same about your instruction. Bonus: Share these observations with other colleagues.

2. Practice focusing on your students' strengths and highlighting those in a classroom version of a reverse pineapple chart.

Acknowledge the Elephant in the Room

Another advantage to acknowledging others' strengths is that it helps you to value one another and yourself and creates a safer environment to share some of the elements of identity that you feel more vulnerable about.

As stated, categorizing people into subgroups is inherently not empathetic and a passive-aggressive form of shaming. On the flipside, to avoid "labeling," many people pretend that diversity doesn't exist ("I don't see color"), which is equally shaming. We must always keep in mind that we all have implicit biases, but we may not be aware of them, and they don't always match up with our intentional beliefs (Singer, 2015).

Microaggressions occur in a misguided effort to forge common ground based on generalizations (e.g., a white person telling a black person that she loves rap music). They also frequently occur when people are not aware that they have a widely held implicit bias that the norm is white, heterosexual, cisgender, abled, Christian. In fact, many nonwhite, heterosexual, cisgender, abled Christians see someone other than themselves as the norm.

The thing is that the vast majority of Americans do not fit all criteria for the "norm." But some of us can hide our identities better than others. As a Jewish American, I am often reluctant to share with people that I am Jewish (in fact, I've spent over an hour just writing this paragraph). Or, when I do, I minimize it ("I'm Jewish, but not practicing, and my husband is Catholic").

Why am I so hesitant to share that I am Jewish? Because I know what other people think when they hear the word. Members of any marginalized groups are well-aware of stereotypes, generalizations, and associations about our groups. We recognize that others may hold these beliefs as truths or are not cognizant of or deny their implicit biases, and we are afraid of the microaggressions that result from these unconscious biases. Because when microaggressions are made toward us, we feel *shame.*

In addition to protecting myself from feeling shame, I learned to hide from this aspect of my identity to avoid potentially tarnishing what someone may think of me. Similarly, I have friends who don't share their sexual orientation, mental illness, or socioeconomic status freely. This is a result of learned shame.

Nonverbal communication, including silence, can also be a form of microaggression. One might comment, "I wasn't sure if he was Jewish (or gay), so I didn't say anything because I didn't want to inadvertently offend him." Examine this with an empathy lens. If you are afraid to ask someone who is not Jewish or gay if they *are* because you don't want to offend them, you are implicitly stating that being Jewish or gay is offensive. You are *shaming* people for parts of their identity that they were born with, rather than *empathizing*—and ultimately seeing the world with rich, diverse perspectives.

It often feels right for us to ignore things or beat around the bush, but let me ask a question: How empathetic is it to *ignore* that someone is Jewish, gay, or homeless? Do you think they don't know they are Jewish, gay, or homeless? So, if you don't say anything, they won't know they are?

Now, let's look at this through the lens of marginalized groups of people who cannot "hide in plain sight" (e.g., Asians, blacks, women). A few years back, I attended a problem-solving team meeting for a team of 7th grade teachers. The team was discussing a particular student and brainstorming potential interventions. One of the strategies that the team wanted to try was praising the student for appropriate behavior during unstructured time (e.g., recess, passing periods, arrival, and dismissal). One of the teachers on the team was a hallway supervisor but did not have this student in her class. She said, "I don't know who Joey [not his real name] is." Another teacher responded, "He's close to 6 feet tall. Got black hair. He wears thick-rimmed glasses." The hallway supervisor still looked puzzled.

At this point, another teacher on the team, who happened to be Asian, said, "He's Asian."

The hallway supervisor immediately said, "Oh! I know who you are talking about!"

All of the other teachers on the team looked stunned.

The Asian teacher said, "there is nothing wrong with using the word *Asian* to describe someone. Joey *is* Asian. You all act as if using the word *Asian* to describe someone's appearance is the same as using the word *Asian* to describe someone's math ability. It's not."

This conversation stuck with me for a long time because it was such a powerful, eye-opening learning experience. One teacher said, "I'm sorry. I wasn't sure if *Asian* was the appropriate term or if I should be saying Korean, Japanese, or whatever." This is the first way you can recognize the elephant in the room: ask someone what the best way is to refer to a group of people and acknowledge the reason you are asking (because you are unsure of the right way and want to make sure you don't ignore a group or offend them by using an inappropriate term).

You must get more comfortable with our collective differences and our own differences. As with everything, you must empathize with yourself first.

It is almost certain that you belong to at least one marginalized group or have a close friend or family member who does. It may feel uncomfortable to ask people questions about their race, religion, gender identification, and so on, but asking yourself why you are uncomfortable can help you tap into the root of your discomfort. It is quite possible you are projecting your own discomfort about parts of your identity onto someone else instead of sharing in the common feelings that are the root of empathy and equity. You must recognize that we are all human and that "norms" do not apply when it comes to humans. By starting the dialogue, you will build resilience around your own shame triggers and have more compassion for yourself and others.

 Read and Reflect

Read the vignette from Dr. Carol L. Kelley, a former superintendent of Oak Park Elementary School District 97 in Oak Park, Illinois, as she reflects on the empathy and equity in school systems from her vantage point of being a woman of color, a mother, and a leader of a large, diverse school system. What parts of her perspective confirm something you already thought? What aspects of her perspective push you to think about things differently? How did open dialogue promote empathy and equity in Kelley's school system?

Empathy and Equity in One School District
By Dr. Carol L. Kelley

When Lisa emailed to ask if I would be interested in writing a vignette about my experience as a superintendent leading for equity and the role empathy plays in that, I wondered what I could share, especially now.

You see, over the past five years during my tenure as superintendent of Oak Park Elementary School District 97, local and national events have hurt my heart, to the point where I have questioned my efficacy as a leader, where I have questioned the efficacy of our profession with achieving equity. The tragic and preventable deaths of George Floyd, Breonna Taylor, Ahmaud Arbery, and many others were painful, visible reminders of the deep, systemic racism that persists across so many of our nation's institutions, including our schools. In my grief as a mother of two black sons, an educational leader, and a woman of color, I frankly wondered if the equity efforts we have initiated in my school community over the past five years would be enough to help dismantle the white supremacy culture found in our schools.

As I thought about what I might share in this vignette, I was reminded of one of my favorite quotes by Margaret Wheatley:

"Very great change starts from very small conversations, held among people who care."

At the start of my Oak Park tenure, I engaged the community in a two-way dialogue to co-construct our current vision that integrated the community's collective values and wisdom: *"Create positive learning environments that are equitable, inclusive, and focused on the whole child."* Our framework for action is a "work-in-progress" approach, where we continually engage in improvement, feedback, evaluation, and adjustment. In essence, we have reversed the traditional sequence of "plan the work and work the plan" by beginning with small-scale actions designed to get a firmer grip on the equity problem we are trying to address, what may work and why (or why not), and what areas require further development. As this work unfolded, we built in opportunities to listen to and learn from the very people most affected by our equity challenges and who could assess how effective our actions have been with addressing the identified equity challenge. Here is one example of what this looks like.

Through ongoing conversations I've had with our students, I've learned that our African American students are not experiencing a strong sense of belonging in our schools, nor are they receiving access to equitable educational experiences in our schools as demonstrated by student learning data, discipline data, and student survey data.

In an effort to better understand the perspectives on the needs and interests of our students and families, I decided to host a series of focus groups, or "empathy interviews." One of these conversations, I will never forget. I sent personal invitations to each 4th grade African American student in my district (and permitted them to bring a parent) for an evening of pizza and conversation. On a cold, wintry school night, close to 20 students (most with a parent) filed into the library of one of our elementary schools to meet with me and several members of my "design team." Following a quick welcome, I reviewed the purpose of the evening and then split everyone into two groups—one for parents and one for students. For 90 minutes, we asked both groups to describe their experiences to us.

What did we learn from listening with empathy? A lot. And, from our learning we were better able to plan. We were able to communicate that our plan would be based on what we heard from our students and parents and not the other way around. Since this initial empathy interview occurred, I have hosted several similar events, and so have other members of our administrative team, as well as several of our teachers.

In terms of concrete actions that we have tried and tested based on the feedback from our empathy interviews, there have been many, including

- Ensuring challenging, culturally responsive curriculum and teaching for our students.
- Emphasizing our focus on social-emotional supports (e.g., increased the number of counselors and social workers, instituted trauma-informed practices, followed social justice standards).
- Increasing efforts to recruit and retain a diverse staff.
- Expanding inclusive teaching practices, including co-teaching and differentiation.
- Disrupting the notion of discipline as punitive and shifting to restorative practices.
- Adding Positive Culture Climate coaches—one at each middle school and two for the elementary schools.
- Expanding concepts like advisory and morning meetings, with a focus on social-emotional issues beyond the SEL curriculum that we had already put in place.

In summary, as I think of empathy, the ability to understand and share the feelings of others, I recognize that these empathy interviews play a vital and valuable role in setting the course for equitably educating our children.

And if we are going to stand in solidarity against acts of racism and inequitable treatment of all people, moments like this must occur more often. Taking the time to listen to others' experiences and using that information to plan our school and district agendas is the foundation necessary for changing our schools and districts for the better. My hope is that we can all do this work together, regardless of what role you play in education, so that children in Oak Park and communities across the county will have very different experiences related to race and injustice.

Culturally Empathetic Curriculum and Instructional Design

I discussed the intersection of empathy and curriculum in Chapter 2, but culturally responsive instruction specifically is a hot topic in education. *Culturally responsive* is defined as a pedagogy that recognizes the importance of including students' cultural references in all aspects of learning (Burnham, 2020). Culturally empathetic curriculum and instruction take cultural responsiveness one step further by addressing and strengthening the three facets of empathy—affective, cognitive, and behavioral—through all aspects of learning.

Below are some examples of how to address and foster the specific components of cultural empathy through curriculum and instructional design.

Build Emotional Empathy Through Literature

"Fiction is empathy's gateway drug," says empathy researcher and author Jamil Zaki in his book *The War for Kindness* (2019, p. 82). Literature, as he shares, is portable, discreet, and is proven to grow readers' empathy toward others, especially people who are unlike them (pp. 82–85). This is corroborated by scientific research conducted in 2013 by the New School in New York City, which found that those who read more literature scored higher when inferring others' feelings than participants who did not read as much literature (Riess, 2018, p.133).

English Language Arts and Curriculum and Instruction departments often fervently debate literature choices. Teams find themselves at a crossroads as they struggle to find consensus when answering questions like, *"Do we eliminate all of the classic literature we've always taught because it's primarily written by white authors?" "What about books that paint nonwhite characters in an unfavorable light?"* and *"What novels do the best jobs representing different cultures?"*

I believe the answer to these questions (as with almost everything) is somewhere in the middle. Concentrate less on the novel selection, and more on the standards you will use to assess mastery. If you choose the correct standards, (for example, RL.3/RI.3, which focuses on characters or individuals; RL.6/RI.6, which focuses on point of view and perspective; or simply RL.1/RI.1, which asks students to use text evidence to support a claim), you can use almost any high-quality piece of literature (classic, contemporary, or culturally diverse) as a vehicle to increase comprehension as well as increase empathy.

As emphasized in Chapter 2, creating strong learning intentions and success criteria is essential for any high-quality instruction. If you intentionally create success criteria to help students understand characters' emotions, you can use any text to help students see things through the perspective of the characters in the text and, through high-quality questioning, see things from a "nonexistent" character (see an 8th grade example in Figure 4.2).

FIGURE 4.2
8th Grade Example of Learning Intentions and Success Criteria

Focus Standards	Learning Intentions	Success Criteria
RL.8.3 Analyze how particular lines of dialogue or incidents in a story or drama propel the action, reveal aspects of a character, or provoke a decision. **RL.8.1** Cite the textual evidence that most strongly supports an analysis of what the text says explicitly as well as inferences drawn from the text.	1. Analyze particular lines of dialogue. 2. Analyze particular incidents in a story or drama.	1a. Students cite meaningful **dialogue** in literature. 1b. Student analyzes how the meaningful dialogue do one or more of the following: propels **action,** reveals character traits, motivates **character** decisions and support with text evidence. 2a Students cite meaningful **incidents** in literature. 2b. Student analyzes how the particular incidents do one or more of the following: propels **action,** reveals character traits, motivates **character** decisions and support with text evidence. 2c. Using text evidence, student infers how characters' responses or actions may have been different if they were a different race, gender, religion, were adopted, didn't speak English, and so on.

For younger students, the idea is the same: use the standards to intentionally design learning opportunities that allow students to go deeper than surface level by examining text from both the character's point of view and their own (see a 3rd grade example in Figure 4.3).

In any grade level, engaging students in discussion about their answers to questions and comparing and contrasting their points of view about character traits and actions can further cultivate empathic capacity.

FIGURE 4.3
3rd Grade Example of Learning Intentions and Success Criteria

Focus Standards	Learning Intentions	Success Criteria
RL.3.3 Describe characters in a story (e.g., their traits, motivations, or feelings) and explain how their actions contribute to the sequence of events.	1. Describe the characters in (*insert text name here*). 2. Explain how the actions of the character affect the plot of (*insert name here*).	1a. Students use adjectives to describe a character's appearance, character traits, and/or feelings. 1b. Students use verbs to describe a character's motivations. 2a. With evidence from the text, students describe how a character's specific action or trait impacted the other characters or events. 2c. Students determine if they would have responded similarly to or differently from the character and why. Students cite their own personality traits and experiences to support their answers.

Bridge Emotional Empathy and Perspective Taking with Identity Charts

Psychology Today defines *identity* as "the memories, experiences, relationships, and values that create one's sense of self" (2020, para. 1).

The root of shame (again, the antithesis of empathy) is centered in our identities. When an aspect of our identity is threatened, we feel shame. To help students build their empathic capacity, you must design instruction that lets them see things through others' eyes as well as better understand how their own identities shape their personal perspectives.

One strategy that can really help with this is to use identity charts for both students and characters or individuals. Identity charts are graphic organizers that help students visualize and consider the many factors that shape individuals and communities (Facing History and Ourselves, n.d.).

I recommend having students create their own identity chart at the beginning of the year and continue adding or subtracting from the chart (helping students recognize which parts of their identity are fluid and which are fixed).

Then, as you introduce pieces of literature or begin a study of an individual or culture, have students (individually or collaboratively) create identity charts for characters, people, or groups of people. In a safe and empathetic way, encourage sharing and discussion of both personal and nonpersonal identity charts as a means to induce empathy and reduce "othering." One way to do this is to model vulnerability first by sharing your own identity chart (including the parts of your identity that you are sometimes hesitant to share). I have witnessed teachers modeling the identity chart exercise, and it is both a powerful learning tool and opportunity to forge a connection through common ground—humanity in both its magnificence and vicissitude. To practice what I preach, I am sharing my own identity chart in Figure 4.4.

FIGURE 4.4
Lisa's Identity Chart

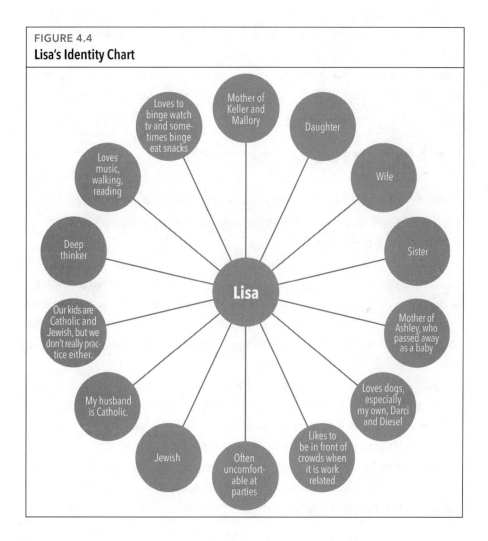

You can also use identity charts in history and social studies classes to help students empathize with and take the perspective of different people or groups of people throughout history. Doing two identity charts side-by-side can help students see the perspectives of others. In October 2020, during COVID-19 and right before the heated 59th U.S. presidential election, I observed an 8th grade social studies teacher use this technique with her virtual class. The students mirrored American society at large because they were split 50/50 in terms of ardent support of one candidate or the other. Because this was a social studies class and some of the content covered government topics, the class would frequently erupt in fierce debates, and students were struggling to empathize with those who had different political views from them.

The class engaged in some research and then created identity charts for Donald Trump, Mike Pence, Joe Biden, and Kamala Harris. These charts became anchors for future conversations about who these people were, why some of the class might identify more with one candidate over another, and so on. Through this process, the students were better able to see their classmates' perspectives, and the classroom quickly became less divisive and more objective.

Increase Perspective Taking with Artistic Expression

Like literature, art in any form (e.g., imagery, music, sculpture) is also a gateway to building empathy. "Art can move an empathic idea from the emotional into the cognitive. When art evokes a strong enough emotion, we want to share that experience, often inspiriting words and actions" (Riess, 2018, p. 132).

Turkish artist Uğur Gallenkus has collections of photo montages that illustrate two perspectives of the same thing side by side, making dramatic impressions on viewers. It is worth noting that some of Gallenkus's photos are exceptionally provocative or graphic and certainly not appropriate for students. Many images, however, can serve as almost instant cognitive empathy (perspective taking) prompts. For example, Gallenkus has one photo in which two groups of women form a straight line: the first half of the line is fashion models walking the catwalk, which bleeds into the second half of the line comprising refugee mothers and their children walking to safety (Uptas, 2018).

Using art and questioning with intentionality can lead to students' greater respect and understanding of others' perspectives. You can use any art form; I particularly find photography and music, in addition to literature, to be the most effective media. A number of recent studies out of Southern Methodist

University (2018) have suggested that empathy is related to the intensity of emotional responses to music, listening style, and musical preferences—for example, empathic people are more likely to enjoy sad music.

So, perhaps having students analyze the lyrics of a song in social studies or having students explore why a musician chose specific instruments or beat or rhythm (in music class) can grow empathy in students who may not choose to listen to sad music on their own time.

A spin on this is to have students share music or photographs or other art pieces that resonate with them and share why. Helen Riess (2018) points out that to move from affective (emotional) to cognitive (perspective taking) empathy, one must be compelled to share with others.

During the COVID-19 pandemic, I saw a creative example of an interdisciplinary learning opportunity that combined art learning intentions, geometry learning intentions, and student innovation to create projects with items students had at home. This opportunity led to both academic and empathic growth for students as they gained insight into their classmates' lives while learning the difference between types of angles and lines.

Also during the pandemic, I had the pleasure of working with a team of 2nd grade teachers at Holmes Primary School in Clarendon Hills, Illinois, who used art as a springboard to build empathy for their students and themselves. They provided a great example of using art and questioning to help students identify others' emotions (affective empathy) and see things from others' perspective (cognitive empathy).

While teaching remotely via Zoom in the fall of 2020, the teachers began their morning meeting by showing their students a photograph from 1940 during a polio outbreak. The picture showed four students of varying ages (likely siblings) gathered around a radio listening to a lesson from their teacher. The students were dressed formally; some had books and others had notebooks and pencils. The teachers used this photograph as a prompt to ask a variety of thought-provoking questions that elicited some fascinating empathetic responses from the students.

Teacher: What do you think the children are doing in the picture?

Students: They are sitting around something, but I'm not sure what it is. They are reading books and writing something.

Teacher: Is there technology in the picture?

Students: No, they don't have computers.

After the teacher explains what is happening in the picture and what a radio is, there are more questions.

Teacher: Can you tell how the students are feeling?

Students: I think they look happy. They are learning. They want to learn and be together. They are dressed so nicely; they take school seriously. Maybe they feel sad or bored because they aren't in school.

Teacher: When our building closed on March 13 last year, what were you thinking? How were you feeling?

Students: At first, I thought this was amazing because we got to take our [computers] home. But then later, I remember my mom and dad watching the news, and I got scared and worried. I was worried. I was confused wondering when will this ever end? Will it always be like this? We were anxious, bored. We'll get to tell our kids about this someday—that we went to school over Zoom and had to wear masks everywhere we went.

Teacher: How is their remote learning the same or different from yours?

Students: It's the same because they are learning from home! It's different because the students don't have computers. They can't see their teacher. I wonder if they could ever see their friends. We see our friends on Zoom, but they can't see anyone on that radio.

Teacher: Do you think it was easier or harder? Why?

Students: Harder. Those kids are different ages. How does the teacher teach all of them? Are they all learning the same thing? How does the teacher see their work? They probably couldn't ask any questions.

Teacher: How does this picture make you feel?

Students: It makes me feel like we aren't alone. Other students have done this. I didn't know that. It makes me feel grateful we have color photos and more technology! I feel that teaching is as hard as learning.

This lesson not only helped students to build their empathy skills but also gave the teachers insight into how the students were feeling and what might be going on in their worlds. This insight then allowed the teachers to respond more empathetically to students and be mindful of their students' perspectives when they planned subsequent lessons.

> **Reflect:** What is a song (or any piece of art) that really resonates with you? Why? What do you feel when you listen to (or look at) this art? Who created the piece? What do you think that person's original message was?

> **Try This:** Create your own identity chart. Identify what parts of your identity are fixed and what parts are fluid. Are there any parts of your identity that were difficult for you to put down on paper? Why do you think this is?

Generate Behavioral Empathy with Problem-Based Learning and STEM

There has been an explosion of STEM (science, technology, engineering, and mathematics) programs in K–12 education in recent years. STEM programs and the advent of tools like 3-D printers have allowed students to innovate in ways they have never been able to in the past. I have seen some remarkable creations (e.g., designing prosthetic limbs for amputees). Moreover, I have seen some incredible lesson designs that began with teachers proactively planning empathetic instruction to avoid unintentionally shaming or making assumptions about their students and resulted in enriching opportunities that stretched student learning.

For example, I once worked with a team of 5th grade teachers who were writing a curriculum for their new STEM program. The team initially designed a project that required students to create a skateboard for someone who has a disability. But something about this project was bothering some members of the team. Specifically, one teacher said, "I'm wondering if this project is insensitive or offensive to a student who has a disability or who has a family member who has a disability."

I asked why the teacher thought it might be insensitive or offensive, and the teacher responded, "Because it points out their disability. They may feel embarrassed."

"Does the person know they have a disability that prevents them from riding a skateboard?" I asked.

"Yes, of course," the teacher responded.

I inquired further, "Do you know if riding a skateboard is something the person would like to do?"

The teacher said, "No, actually, I don't."

This is a concrete example of potentially empathizing with someone on an affective (emotional) level but failing to empathize with them on a cognitive (perspective taking) level. You may see a person with a disability who cannot join in an abled person's activity and assume you have correctly identified that person's emotion as sad or envious. But without engaging in dialogue to confirm what the other person is feeling, you are imposing your perspective (*I would want to skateboard, too*) and then acting accordingly (*design something to simulate a skateboarding experience*).

A more empathetic approach is what this team of teachers wound up doing: identifying people with disabilities for their *strengths* and empathizing with the uncontrollable *deficits* the person may have.

The team of teachers wound up forming teams of students (three to four per group) and had each group partner with a student with a physical disability from their educational community. The students began their STEM project by just getting to know one another, spending time playing games, interacting, and building authentic relationships. Then, they engaged in interviews with the students. Each student in the group (disabled or not) had an opportunity to ask and answer interview questions:

1. What is your favorite pastime or hobby? Why?
2. What is one of your strengths that you are proud of? Why?
3. What is something that frustrates you? Why?
4. What could potentially lessen this frustration for you?

In the end, the STEM groups designed assistive tools that were inspired by the students for whom they were created to solve an authentic problem each student faced. Many of the problems had nothing at all to do with a disability. They were things like, "It frustrates me when my sister barges into my room without knocking, but my mom won't let me have a lock on my bedroom door." The students wound up designing a device that sensed movement and said, "Don't forget to knock," when anyone approached the door.

In this process, the students involved learned about others' strengths, their strengths, and how these strengths complemented one another.

Reflect:
- What is a strength of yours that you are proud of? Why?
- What is something that frustrates you? Why?
- What could potentially lessen this frustration for you?
- Who might be a good person to partner with to explore ways to alleviate this frustration?

Intention and Response

Even with the best intentions, the most proactive approaches, and the most refined empathic skill, there are times when you will "miss," especially when you are experiencing times of personal distress. When you overlook something, inadvertently embarrass or shame someone, or fail to empathize completely, what remains in our control is how you respond.

The key to restoring any injury to a relationship through a microaggression or other empathic misstep is to remain reflective and objective. In reflecting on situations where you (intentionally or unintentionally) hurt, shamed, or dismissed someone or a group of people, the best thing to do (as illustrated in Chapter 3) is to own your part and apologize sincerely without getting defensive and causing a power struggle in which no one wins. This is a skill that takes practice and one that (because you are human) you will have an opportunity to practice quite a bit.

One thing that can help you remain reflective and intentional is to spend some time thinking about the students you serve and some of the factors that may arouse your implicit bias, causing you to be extra mindful of how you empathize with these students. Figure 4.5 can be a helpful tool to document your reflection and intention.

Try This: With a colleague or team of colleagues, use the chart in Figure 4.5 to brainstorm "othering" considerations that are prominent parts of your students' identities (some examples are listed). Then, brainstorm look-fors for both students and teachers in columns two and three.

FIGURE 4.5
Identifying "Othering" in Your Class

Identity Consideration Ex: Gender Identification/ Sexual Orientation; Race; Religion/Culture; English Language Learners; Physical Disability; Learning Difference/Special Education	In a classroom that is empathetic to this factor, I would see and hear <u>students</u>:	In a classroom that is empathetic to this factor, I would see and hear <u>teachers</u>:

5

Empathetic Instruction and Assessment Strategies

More than half of the United States have regulations or mandates to provide social-emotional learning for students. This encompasses character programs, mindfulness programs, antibullying programs, emotional regulation programs, and more (Gabriel, Harper, Steed, & Temkin, 2019). Studies show that SEL programs are effective and that participating students better understand one another's feelings and have increased self-regulation strategies. Additionally, systems see less bullying, fewer disciplinary issues, and improved academic performance. However, these studies also find that these results are only effective with younger students. When students are teenagers, starting these programs has little to no impact (Zaki, 2019, p. 140). This data show us two significant things: (1) the younger students are, the greater the opportunity to positively influence their ability to empathize, and (2) having an SEL curriculum is not enough. In addition to any programs, teachers must model empathy implicitly and explicitly so that students can experience empathy and grow more empathetic in real time. This chapter outlines several ways you can do this within the construct of a typical school day using instruction and assessment practices rather than or in addition to any formal SEL program.

We start to develop the skill of empathy at birth by the bonds we make with our primary caregivers. Children acquire empathy through modeling, similar to speech. Dependable nurturing from consistent caregivers leads to higher empathetic capacity in children. Conversely, a lack of consistent nurturing can (but not always) lead to children who don't feel what others feel and, more troublesome, can't yet understand why they should care (because they have not experienced compassion themselves). However, as emphasized throughout this book, we can grow more empathetic; it is not a static trait. Early attachment problems can be attenuated by consistent, nurturing relationships later in life (Szalavitz & Perry, 2010). Even one relationship like this can have a marked effect on children's ability to empathize—relationships like those with teachers.

It can be disarming to think that empathy is learned before we are even conscious of it. It is natural to think of our upbringing and, if you are a parent, to think of how you cared for your children as infants. What was our experience? What were we like when we entered kindergarten? For some children, kindergarten is the first opportunity they have with a consistent caregiver. The nurturing part is where our empathic skills as educators come into play.

Start with Self-Reflection

I venture to guess that at some point, if not multiple times in their careers, all teachers have felt inadequate, aggravated, anxious, and other undesirable feelings. It is how you respond to these feelings that determine if they are temporary or permanent.

I once consulted with a school whose kindergarten teacher exemplified consistency and nurturing. This teacher—let's call her Ms. Smith—was exceptional at setting clear expectations for learning and behavior while allowing each student to shine or safely "fail." Other teachers in the building would often observe Ms. Smith and her interactions with students because she was able to find ways to ensure even the most challenging of students were successful academically, socially, and emotionally. Ms. Smith's class ran like a well-oiled machine, and these students were just 5 years old!

A few months into the second year of my partnership with this school, Ms. Smith gave birth to her first child and took her maternity leave for the remainder of the year. It proved to be a harder year for Ms. Smith; a few of her students presented with more significant academic and social-emotional needs. She was diligent in her approach to meeting her students' needs and quickly partnered with an instructional coach to explore additional strategies to ensure her students' success. When it came time for Ms. Smith to go on her maternity leave, the problematic behaviors of some of her students (e.g., hitting others, leaving the classroom unescorted, and refusing to do work) had all but disappeared. Before Ms. Smith went on leave, she worked closely with her substitute—let's call her Ms. Jones—to onboard her and model all of her systems and structures. Ms.

Smith, her coach, and colleagues felt confident that transitioning to a long-term sub would be seamless.

This was not at all the case. Within days of Ms. Smith's leave, the same behaviors appeared. Except, this time, it wasn't just the three students who presented initially with these actions. Multiple students now refused to do work, didn't ask permission to leave the classroom, and acted aggressively toward one another and Ms. Jones. Plus, there wasn't a day that went by without a student saying, "Ms. Smith didn't do it like that" or asking, "When is Ms. Smith coming back?"

Many days ended with both Ms. Jones and students fighting back tears. What in the world was happening? In short, empathy was absent on the part of both the students and the teacher.

Many of the students were unable to empathize with the substitute's frustration for various reasons, including that they were just 5 years old and their empathic skills were still emerging. In addition, for students who had experienced or were experiencing trauma (whether the trauma was documented or not), Ms. Smith's "leaving" was a trigger event. *Someone I love has left me.* As discussed in Chapter 3, trauma triggers create the same feelings that students felt during their initial trauma: fear, confusion, abandonment, shame, and so on. In turn, these feelings often manifest in a variety of undesirable or unsafe behaviors.

The teacher herself was also experiencing shame, which left her feeling disconnected from her students and herself. *These students don't like me. I'm a terrible teacher. I'll never be as good as Ms. Smith. The principal/coach/parents should have given me more training and time.*

So, what do you do in situations like this? In short, empathize. And begin by empathizing with yourself.

Focus on your feelings and why you feel that way. Validate your feelings—it's OK to feel however you feel. Ask yourself what is causing you to feel that way? Focus on specific reasons (e.g., things that, with help, you can control) and avoid negative self-talk or blaming (e.g., defeating statements or looking outward on things you cannot control). Figure 5.1 demonstrates this reflective process using the substitute, Ms. Jones, as an example.

Model Empathy with Cooperative Learning Structures and Read-Alouds

After engaging in this reflective process, Ms. Jones met with a trusted instructional coach (a colleague would work, too) to help her see things more clearly

---

FIGURE 5.1
Self-Reflection Tool: Ms. Jones

Step 1: Identify Your Emotions (affective empathy)	Step 2: Validate Your Feelings (cognitive empathy)	Step 3: Focus on What You Can Control and Set a Goal (behavioral empathy)
Honestly answer the question: *How do I feel?*	Answer the question: *What are the reasons I feel this way?*	Look back at your responses in Step 2 and code them as follows: • Is this something within your control? If so, **highlight your response.** • Is this reason negative self-talk? If so, ~~strike~~ your answer. • Is this reason placing outward blame? If so, ~~strike~~ your answer.
Inadequate	I'm upset because my students keep asking when Ms. Smith is coming back, and I want them to see me as their teacher. ~~I'm upset I'll never be like Ms. Smith.~~	
Frustrated/Aggravated	It frustrates me that I spend a lot of time planning solid lessons and then my students don't participate in class. ~~It aggravates me that parents don't do a better job making sure their kids listen to their teachers.~~	
Nervous/Anxious	I'm nervous that an administrator will walk into my room and think I have poor classroom management. ~~I'm nervous because admin didn't give me enough training.~~	

My goal: I want my students to see me as their teacher.

and determine an action plan for meeting her goal of the students accepting her as their teacher. Together the coach and teacher chose two strategies: using cooperative learning structures and standards-aligned read-alouds.

The first step in this action plan was for the teacher to be vulnerable with her students and model empathy for both herself and her students' perspectives. She started by introducing a cooperative learning structure at her morning meeting time, which had become one of the most dreaded parts of her day because it was nearly impossible for her to gain the students' attention. She used the same song that Ms. Smith used to signal that everyone should put their things away and be seated in their spots by the time the song ended. But, inevitably, the song would end, and more than half of the students would still be doing other things. As a result, Ms. Jones raised her voice or resorted to bargaining with students to come to the carpet.

So, Ms. Jones changed tactics. She used the same song, but instead of raising her voice when the song ended, she sat on the carpet with the students who were there and said, "Some of our friends need a little bit of extra time, so we will get started, and they will join us when they are ready."

It took a bit of time, but eventually, all of the students came to the carpet. At this point, Ms. Jones stopped and said, "Boys and girls, I owe you an apology. I realized that I felt very frustrated at the start of our day when our morning meeting started late. Do you know what *frustrated* means?"

A few students raised their hands and gave answers like "annoyed," "angry because you can't do something," and "tired." Ms. Jones praised their answers and then asked, "Have you ever felt frustrated? Raise your hand if you have." Almost everyone raised their hand, and Ms. Jones instructed the students to turn and talk to their shoulder partners and share something that frustrates them. "You have one minute to talk, and when I raise my hand, please stop talking and raise your hand, too." Ms. Jones held her breath. But, sure enough, the structure worked. Within a few seconds of raising her hand, the students did, too. And, she had their attention.

Now, Ms. Jones said, "I heard some great conversations. Annie, can you tell me what frustrates your partner?"

Annie said, "It frustrates Kyle when his little brother takes his toys."

Ms. Jones replied, "Oh, I can imagine how frustrated you feel. I have three younger brothers, and I remember feeling frustrated when they took my LEGOs! When I would get frustrated when I was a kid like you, I sometimes would slam my door, which wasn't the best strategy for me. I needed to find a better way to respond to my frustration. What do you do when you feel frustrated?"

Ms. Jones continued the morning meeting with a series of turn-and-talks to both model what empathy looks like and help grow their personal, empathic skills. Before this conversation, many of the students had not correctly identified what Ms. Jones felt when they were late to the meeting. They didn't have the ability yet to see her perspective; first, they had to connect to their own feelings. Exercises where a teacher models feelings, point of view, and actions can help students read emotions and see others' perspectives.

The other strategy Ms. Jones and her coach chose to use was standards-aligned read-alouds. As discussed in Chapter 4, reading literature is proven to increase our empathic ability. Conducting read-alouds with children who are emerging readers (and even for proficient readers in smaller doses) allows teachers and students to tap into the power of literature to elicit empathy.

But before Ms. Jones could implement the read-aloud strategy, she needed to empathize with her students' feelings about Ms. Smith. She began the literature lesson by giving each student a set of laminated emoji cards and putting a picture of Ms. Smith up on the Smart Board. The students reacted as Ms. Jones anticipated with ooohs and ahhs—a reaction that previously would have intimidated her. Instead, this day, she empathized, "I can see this picture is getting quite the reaction! I imagine you all feel something when you see Ms. Smith. Do you know how you feel right now? Hold up the emoji that best represents how the picture makes you feel."

Many students held up a happy face, some held up the sad face, a few mad, and one student the confused card. The students turned and talked about their feelings. Through this instructional strategy, Ms. Jones understood the multiple perspectives her students had about Ms. Smith's departure. She then was able to respond compassionately toward them by asking targeted questions during their read-aloud.

Ms. Jones started with the learning standard they were addressing in class: CCSS.RL.K.1: "with prompting and support, ask and answer questions." One of the greatest gifts of the Common Core (and other sets of) standards is that they are primarily skill-based. This gives teachers the autonomy to select meaningful text and curriculum. Ms. Jones chose to read the children's book *Same Way Ben*, which is about a little boy whose beloved teacher has a baby and he has to adjust to a teacher who does things a little bit differently than his teacher (Cocca-Leffler, 2019). By instructing and assessing the standard at hand with this intentionally chosen text, the teacher could gain evidence of her students' academic progress while building classroom community through empathy and, ultimately, accomplishing her goal of establishing herself as the class's teacher.

 Try This: Practice empathizing with yourself about something personal or professional. Use the blank chart in Figure 5.2 to guide your reflection.

FIGURE 5.2
Self-Reflection Template

Step 1: Identify Your Emotions (affective empathy)	Step 2: Validate Your Feelings (cognitive empathy)	Step 3: Focus on What You Can Control and Set a Goal (behavioral empathy)
Honestly answer the question: *How do I feel?*	Answer the question: *What are the reasons I feel this way?*	Look back at your responses in Step 2 and code them as follows: • Is this something within your control? If so, **highlight your response.** • Is this reason negative self-talk? If so, ~~strike~~ your answer. • Is this reason placing outward blame? If so, ~~strike~~ your answer.

My goal: _____

Use Formative Assessment

Formative assessment is perhaps the most empathetic instructional practice we can employ in our classrooms and schools because it relies on several inherently empathetic questions: What do my students need in order to learn? How do I know? What will I try to ensure they continue to grow academically, socially, and emotionally? How will I know if what I am trying is working?

Sometimes referred to as assessment for learning, formative assessment is designed to inform both students and teachers of students' progress toward learning targets and focuses on feedback and improvement rather than results and grades (more on that in Chapter 6). Formative assessments are anything that gives teachers evidence to support their instruction and gives students feedback about their relationship to the learning target. Simply put, every time a student practices or attempts a skill, it's a formative assessment. The attempts are meant to sharpen skills until students are proficient in demonstrating the skill or concept.

The evidence from these formative assessments is what drives the feedback teachers give to students. Contrary to popular belief, *assessment* is not synonymous with *test*. In fact, if the test is a multiple-choice format, it is likely not a solid formative assessment because it doesn't give clear insight into a student's relationship to a specific learning target.

In addition, true formative assessment in its organically empathetic state focuses on giving students feedback instead of grades and eliminates the need for the heated discussion on "retakes." There are no retakes, just additional attempts until students reach proficiency. Progress is different for everyone; it's natural, therefore, for some students to need additional opportunities to practice after receiving feedback. This isn't a retake. This is being empathetic to students' learning needs. Not allowing some students additional opportunities because some of their classmates mastered it sooner or because the unit test has always been given on a certain day is the antithesis of empathetic instruction and assessment. From a practical standpoint, keep in mind the following things:

1. You do not need to assess every student the same number of times.
2. You will need to assess some students more frequently than others based on how long it takes them to acquire skills or understanding of concepts.
3. You do not need to assess all students on the same day or at the same time.

Conversely, some students will demonstrate understanding of the content or mastery of a skill early on in a unit of study. It is crucial that you are also empathetic to these students' needs. Sitting in a classroom, bored, day after day leads to apathy toward learning, and if you leave it to these students to point out that they are bored, you risk shaming them because they may be labeled by other students or admonished as "disrespectful." Through formative assessment (including a pre-assessment), however, you can identify these students and plan instruction that extends their learning needs.

Implement Flexible Grouping

When designing instruction, formative assessment evidence allows teachers to group students flexibly rather than grouping them into static ability-level groups (otherwise known as tracking). The goal of flexible grouping is to target specific student needs according to mastery of the predetermined success criteria (examples of rigor). Flexible grouping creates temporary groups for a day, a week, or a month, not an entire semester or year. I recommend using flexible grouping structures after a portion of whole-class direct instruction of new content. Expose all of the students to the new, grade-level or above content, and then, when it is time for students to practice or process their learning, give them opportunities to do so at their readiness level.

Formative assessment and flexible grouping are inherently empathetic to learners' needs and recognize the great variance in how long it takes students to acquire skills or concepts. Punitive measures (like failing grades) and static ability-level grouping are deeply shaming to the students in the low-end groups or with failing grades and significantly increase the likelihood a student in the high-end group will feel deep shame when they inevitably struggle to learn a skill or concept. Figures 5.3, 5.4, and 5.5 illustrate examples of instructional models for flexible grouping. Consider the examples and these guidelines when developing your own flexible grouping:

1. Give students a formative assessment that aligns to the learning intentions and success criteria.
2. Determine targeted student needs (the discrete skills outlined with the learning intentions and success criteria (e.g., addition versus subtraction).
3. Choose a small-group instruction strategy (e.g., differentiated rotating centers, differentiated progressive centers, whole-group with cooperative learning).
4. Instruct and formatively assess students again.
5. Continue for the remainder of the allotted time for the unit of study or until all students have met all success criteria.

Keep in mind, these groups are *flexible* and will change with each unit and within each unit. Inevitably, some students may not meet all success criteria. Keep track of which students still need to demonstrate which skills. You can always (and may need to) reteach some of these skills (especially foundational skills) in subsequent units (more on this in Chapter 6).

FIGURE 5.3

Flexible Grouping Sample: 3rd Grade Math Rotations

3.MD.8 Solve real-world and mathematical problems involving perimeters of polygons, including finding the perimeter given the side lengths, finding an unknown side length, and exhibiting rectangles with the same perimeter and different areas or with the same area and different perimeters.

Times	Zoom w/ Ms. Moore	Work by Yourself	Design Time	Digital Practice
9:00-9:25	Group 1	Group 4	Group 3	Group 2
9:25-9:50	Group 2	Group 1	Group 4	Group 3
9:50-10:15	Group 3	Group 2	Group 1	Group 4
10:15-10:40	Group 4	Group 3	Group 2	Group 1

Group 1: Anaya, Jonny, Angel, Riley, Wyatt: When given all length sizes, determine the perimeter of closed shapes.

Group 2: Scott, Sloane, Alexis, Jacob, Trevor, Rashesh, Joe: When given the perimeter, determine the unknown length of a side.

Group 3: Grace, Eun, Will, Hudson, Martin, Wynesha: Solve real-world problems involving perimeter.

Group 4: Gustav, Katherine, Pamela: Create real-world problems involving perimeter.

Flexible grouping also allows you to change the makeup of groups to give students an opportunity to work in mixed-ability groups with entry points that are aligned to their specific learning needs. Using cooperative learning structures (like the Kagan Structure that's exemplified in Figure 5.6) allows for mixed-ability grouping that is differentiated and adheres to the foundational pieces of cooperative learning: positive interdependence, individual accountability, equal participation, and simultaneous interaction (Kagan & Kagan, 2017).

FIGURE 5.4

Flexible Grouping Sample: 1st Grade Asynchronous "Daily 5"

Focus Standards: Foundational Skills		FS: Reading Literature/ Informational Text		FS: Writing	
RF1.3 Know and apply grade-level phonics and word analysis skills in decoding words. **RF 1.4** Read with sufficient accuracy and fluency to support comprehension.		**RI1.1** Ask and answer questions about key details in a text. **RL.1.1** Ask and answer questions about key details in a text.		**W.1.3** Write narratives in which they recount a well-elaborated event or short sequence of events, include details to describe actions, thoughts, and feelings, use temporal words to signal event order, and provide a sense of closure.	
Monday *Read to Self*	**Tuesday** *Listen to Others*	**Wednesday** *Play Games*	**Thursday** *Virtual Practice*	**Friday** *Writing*	**Anyday** *Student Choice!*
Students record themselves reading a book of their choosing or reading a decodable reader. When students are done reading, they should ask their classmates a question about the text. (RL.1.1).	Students listen to their classmates read their book choice and answer the question they posed (RL1.1).	Tactile work *or* Virtual games (aligned to priority standards or to increase background knowledge) Examples: *List available tools here*	Targeted practice or assessment using available tools Examples: *List available tools here*	Handwriting practice *or* Reader/ writer notebook activity	Students choose an option from the focused standard-aligned menu.

Most important, flexible grouping avoids the unempathetic alternative of *tracking*. Using static high, medium, and low groups (a long-standing practice in U.S. education) does not value individual students' strengths within a content area, nor does it give students the opportunity to excel. Typically, with ability groups, students remain in their tracks for the duration of their school careers,

FIGURE 5.5
Flexible Grouping Sample: 8th grade ELA Station Progressions

CCSS.ELA-LITERACY.RL.8.2 Determine a theme or central idea of a text and analyze its development over the course of the text, including its relationship to the characters, setting, and plot; provide an objective summary of the text.

- **Today I am:** Analyzing how the author Harper Lee draws on themes and patterns in *To Kill a Mockingbird*.
- **So that I can:** Understand how patterns and themes exist and evolve in literature.
- **I know I've got it when:** I can explain a claim with a variety of strong text evidence (both quoted and paraphrased).

Step/Group 1	Step/Group 2	Step/Group 3
Students state a claim that identifies a possible theme of the text.	Students analyze and explain the development of the identified theme through its • relationship to the characters • relationship to the setting • relationship to the plot **with more than one piece of text evidence** directly quoted from the text about a character, the setting, or the plot.	Students analyze and explain the development of the identified theme through its • relationship to the characters • relationship to the setting • relationship to the plot **with at least one inference** (not directly stated in text) about a character, the setting, or the plot.

Note: Students visit only the station that applies to their current level and move to the next one as they show mastery of each success criteria.

FIGURE 5.6
Cooperative Learning Example: Think – Write – Round Robin (8th Grade ELA)

RL.8.3 Analyze how particular lines of dialogue or incidents in a story or drama propel the action, reveal aspects of a character, or provoke a decision.

After listening to the read-aloud of the scene in *Annie*, reread the text on your own and then answer the following questions on your paper. Share in order and pause to give feedback after each of your group mates shares.

Student 1: Identify two of the main characters in this dialogue.

Student 2: Identify a character trait of one of the characters and share the text evidence to support your claim.

Student 3: Identify what actions resulted from the characters' exchange. Share text evidence to support your claim.

Student 4: Infer how both characters are feeling from this dialogue. Share text evidence to support your claim.

plus they begin to identify as these labels, which results in potentially deep shaming and a long-lasting, self-fulfilling prophecy.

 Reflect: How do you formatively assess students? In what ways can you make these practices more empathetic?

 Try This: Try using one of the flexible grouping templates to target your students' specific needs.

Try Spaced Practice Instead of Mass Practice

The following sections of this chapter will undoubtedly stretch your thinking on how to access content and acquire skills in schools. The strategies presented are both empathetic and empirically proven to be more effective for learning retention; however, they threaten some of the long-standing practices that have become commonplace in schools (especially U.S. schools) and are rarely reflected upon for efficacy.

As a freshman in high school, my son shared one morning that he had a physics test. I asked him what it was on, and he said, "I have no idea." I laughed and asked, "Is it on inertia and centrifugal force on an x/y intercept?" He laughed and said, "Yeah, something like that."

But, really, this is no laughing matter. I took (and passed) physics in high school, and my son will likely follow suit, but did we *learn* these concepts?

I recall the terms *inertia* and *centrifugal force*, and I have a vague recollection of what they are (mainly from our field trip to Six Flags at the end of the course), but to be completely honest, I have no idea what either of these concepts mean. And, sadly, I could say the same about pretty much every history, science, and math class I took in high school. For the record, I graduated at the top of my class and was inducted to the National Honor Society, so this isn't about grades. This is about learning.

If learning is defined as skills or concepts that we can apply to life, I certainly did not *learn* a whole lot in high school. Or maybe a more accurate statement is that I didn't *retain* a whole lot of this learning. This is because I engaged in the prescribed learning strategy known as massed practice—that is, memorize, cram, get it all in for the test, and then forget it as soon as it is over.

Memorization is an integral part of learning, just not at the beginning. Memorizing content, routines, or skills becomes second nature through the antithesis of massed practice, which is spaced practice.

Spaced practice allows learners to commit things to memory naturally. In this way, we are being sensitive to our natural way of learning and easing the cognitive load; humans can only learn so much at one time (Brown, McDaniel, & Roediger, 2018). Spaced practice is inherently empathetic.

Some ways you can adjust your instruction from surface (memorization) to deep learning (application of skills) are as follows:

- **Free up cognitive space by giving students factual information** (dates, places, people, definitions, formulas) or allow them to use Google to find these answers. Then, enable and encourage students to rely on these notes to engage in deeper learning with these facts. For example, instead of asking, "What were the three theaters of battle during World War II?" (surface), ask students a higher-level question: "Which of the three theaters of battle during World War II required the most strategic leadership from a general? Why?"

  With this question, students will automatically have to identify the three theaters of battle, but they won't use their cognitive energy to recall the theaters. Instead, they will consult their notes, recall the three theaters with ease, and tend to the deeper content about the theaters. The more students consult these notes, the more those facts are reinforced, leading to retention of the facts and a deeper understanding of the importance of those facts.

- **Separate fluency from application and analysis of content** and use a combination of both in your classroom. Allow students fluency exercises in math and reading (especially in the primary grades) as crucial building blocks of learning. During fluency exercises, assess for individual student growth, not to give grades or to compare students to one another. Fluency is when we give students as much time as necessary to practice foundational skills.

- **Simultaneously, expose students to rich pieces of text and engage them in age-appropriate, real-world problem solving to build their background knowledge,** which is proven to increase reading comprehension more than fluency alone (Korbey, 2020). By doing so, you offer students a combination of both fluency and more in-depth learning experiences. During those deeper learning experiences, free up students' cognitive space by allowing them to use tools like calculators and audio recordings of text. These deeper experiences are focused on exposure to rich text, using critical-thinking skills, and engagement, in contrast to fluency practice, which is solely focused on giving students multiple, spaced opportunities to practice foundational skills.

Over time, regular fluency practice of foundational skills will result in mastery of those essential skills. However, knowing that some students will take longer than others to "get there," there is no reason to wait for students to master all foundational skills before allowing them to participate in more in-depth learning. A good analogy for this is riding a bicycle. Many of us required the assistance of training wheels to learn how to ride a bike. With those training wheels, we could join our friends and family who no longer had training wheels on bike rides. And, in time, we no longer needed the training wheels. We were not forced to ride a stationary bicycle (analogous to preventing students from engaging in richer learning). Nor were we forced to ride a mountain bike uphill without training wheels before we could ride on solid ground without them (analogous to having students perform tasks that are too rigorous for them without assistive tools).

Instead, a combination of fluency exercises and more in-depth learning opportunities with assistive tools and spaced practice will lead to retention of skills.

Try This: Take a look at an assignment that you are giving or have typically given to students in the past. Highlight any surface-level questions. Now, provide students those answers or have them do a Google search or scavenger hunt for them. Next, create one or two deep-level questions for students to answer using the factual information and additional instruction from you.

Realize Time Is Not a Success Criteria

I often recall my first couple of years teaching and my first experiences ensuring students with individualized education plans (IEPs) received the accommodations and modifications they were entitled to by law. Like many teachers, I struggled at times to "keep all of the accommodations and modifications straight." After a couple of years of struggling, I started asking myself questions like, "Why does a student need an IEP to receive *written directions* or *extended time*? Why aren't all students automatically extended these *accommodations*?" The answer to that question is, candidly, a lack of empathy.

Written directions speak to teacher clarity, which, as emphasized in Chapters 2 and 3, is a crucial component of students' academic and social-emotional success and helps us avoid unintentionally shaming students.

Well, not giving students enough time to complete an assessment certainly results in feeling shame. Time limits are for teachers' convenience, related primarily to grading and returning assignments. If you aim to empathize with students, why would you add a success criterion (time) that is not aligned to the learning standard? To review, success criteria are the measures we use to see if students show the proficiency of the learning intentions that are derived from standards. No standards (that I know of) indicate students must demonstrate all or part of the standard in minutes, hours, days, or months. In fact, standards detail what students should master by the end of the school year.

When you tell students "quiz on Friday" or "you have 40 minutes to complete this," you are adding a success criterion that is not related to the standard. Now, I imagine you're thinking, "But this isn't the real world. We have standardized tests." And you are right, but consider two things. First, in K–12 education, many standardized tests do not have a time limit (e.g., NWEA-MAP) or give all students a copious amount of time (e.g., PARCC). In addition, the college admission scandals in recent years have shone a spotlight on the equity issues stemming from students with more financial means securing extra time for tests through private evaluation. Many tests, like the SATs, are reviewing their practices and procedures.

Second, Spoiler Alert: Finishing a test faster does not correlate to any greater gains later in life. In a fascinating start to season four of Malcolm Gladwell's podcast *Revisionist History*, the first two episodes, entitled "Puzzle Rush" and "The Tortoise and the Hare" respectively, shed a lot of light on this phenomenon.

In episode one, Gladwell (2019a) presents an analogy: the LSATs (which are timed) and the game of chess, which has timed and untimed versions. Chess, depending on which version is being played (puzzle rush versus standard), requires players to use different strategies to win. In puzzle rush, the strategy is beating the clock, not necessarily having the most strategic knowledge of the game. Gladwell proposed that the same holds true for the LSAT, which determines who gets into law school and who does not. This exam is notorious for being difficult, predominantly because of the way the questions are weighted and because it intentionally gives students a limited amount of time. Students will not have enough time to finish the test unless they have a strategy to do so (e.g., skip questions, guess/don't guess).

After taking the LSAT himself and conducting extensive research and interviews, Gladwell's findings are fascinating. Where one goes to law school does not matter. The school someone attended is not a predictor of success in the legal field (Gladwell, 2019b). Knowing that how quickly one takes the LSAT (i.e., indicative of strategizing about time, not necessarily depth of understanding) is one of the main criteria the elite law schools use for entrance, yet attending those schools does not correlate to greater success as a lawyer, we can see that time is not a success criterion.

Gladwell also interviews William Henderson, a firefighter turned lawyer and law professor at Indiana University. As a teacher, Henderson quickly observed his students' stress levels during timed tests and often couldn't assess their understanding of the content. So, he started giving students take-home tests and told them that they had four hours to take it, that they wouldn't need four hours, but that they could take all of that time if they wanted.

After the first take-home exam, one student sought Henderson out about his grade. The student shared that he had been at Indiana University for three years, and he had never done so well on any exam. He had never been more than average. Now, the student wondered if he would have done better if all of his exams had been structured this way. Professor Henderson showed great empathy for his students by sharing their perspectives (timed tests are stressful) and focusing on the success criteria (those not related to time) of the assessments.

To quote Gladwell,

> You have a student who this system declared was of average ability. The student believed it. Why wouldn't he? But then someone came along— someone, by the way, with the great benefit of being a firefighter from the suburbs of Cleveland who had the freedom to think a little differently— and he said, "Wait. Maybe you aren't of average ability. Maybe you only think you're average because we have chosen an arbitrary system to evaluate your ability. That makes you look average." (2019a)

Reflect: Where is time a success criterion in your classroom? Weekly spelling tests? Timed tests? Inflexible due dates? What changes can you make to be more empathetic to all students, not just those who qualify for extended time?

Create Shared Experiences

"Use the group to change the group." This is one of my favorite quotes by author Michael Fullan (Thiers, 2017, para. 22). The same thing can be said for nurturing empathy within a classroom. By using the group's collective perspectives and experiences, teachers can address both students' academic needs and their need for belonging through shared learning experiences.

Shared learning experiences should use authentic examples of content relevant to students' lives as hooks for learning, topics for discussions, and ways to make seemingly "dry" content "sticky." Following are some strategies I've seen teachers use masterfully in their classrooms to create shared learning experiences.

Magic Bag

The "magic bag" is a take on number talks that both makes the number talk "real" and helps students get to know one another. I originally saw this in a 3rd grade classroom, and since then, I've shared with other teachers and seen successful iterations with kindergartners through 12th grade (where it was called "my future bag").

In the original 3rd grade classroom, the teacher began the school year by asking each student to bring something that's special to them to school and placing it in her magic bag. The teacher tells students this can be anything. Some examples:

- A memory from a vacation.
- A picture from their favorite TV show that they download from the internet.
- A stuffed animal.
- A coin.
- A hat.
- Anything appropriate for school.

The teacher then uses those items to begin their number talks, which they had several times a week. The teacher always keeps in mind the learning intention knowing that she will create a number talk based on whatever she picks from the magic bag. (*Tip: As you become more comfortable with this strategy, you may look at the items in the bag ahead of time to prepare the discussion, and then peek when you select the item in front of the students.*) When I observed the class, the learning intention was to solve two-step word problems using the four operations. The teacher chose a photograph of Niagara Falls from the bag. Here's how the conversation went:

Teacher: I'm selecting an item from our magic bag now. What will it be? Here it is. Oh, it looks like a picture of a beautiful waterfall. Whose item it this?

Student (Abby): That is my picture.

Teacher: Thank you for sharing this with us, Abby. Can you tell us what this is a picture of and why it is special to you?

Abby: Yes. My family and I went to Niagara Falls last summer. We rented a really cool minivan because my grandma and grandpa came, too, and it was a lot of fun.

Teacher: Wow, Abby, I can see why this trip was special to you. (To the other students) Boys and girls, have you heard of Niagara Falls before? Does anyone know where Niagara Falls is?

After a show of hands, the teacher calls on a student.

Student: It's in Canada.

Teacher: Yes, that's correct. Thank you!

Abby: Actually, it's in Canada and New York. We went to the New York part because we don't have passports.

Teacher: Oh, that's interesting. I've never been outside of the United States myself, but I would love to go to Italy one day because I love art and architecture. OK, everyone, in a minute, please turn and talk to your shoulder partner. If you've been to another country, share that experience. If you've never been to another country, share a country you think you may like to visit and why. You have a total of two minutes to talk, one minute each. Partner A will speak first, and I will let you know when it's time to switch. Any questions? OK, go!

After two minutes . . .

Teacher: Thank you, students! I heard some great conversations. I heard Isabella share about Venezuela, where she was born, and where there are also waterfalls. I also heard Joshua share that he wants to visit France because he loves French food. I love learning more about all of you! Now, let's talk math! Abby, can I ask you a few questions about your trip?

Abby: Yes!

Teacher: You said you drove there and that your grandparents went with you, correct?

Abby: Yes.

Teacher: Who else went with you?

Abby: My mom, my dad, and my sister.

Teacher: Who drove the minivan?

Abby: My dad drove the whole way there. But then he got tired of driving, so on the way home, my grandpa and my mom drove a little bit.

Teacher: I see. So, you had three drivers. One drove all of one way and 1/3 of the way back. Is there a volunteer willing to Google how far it is from New York City to Niagara Falls, New York? You can round to the nearest whole number.

Student Volunteer: It is approximately 409 miles from New York City to Niagara Falls, New York.

From that point, the teacher continues the number talk, focusing again on the learning intention of solving two-step word problems using the four operations. But with the added bag component, the teacher has made the word problem relevant: "How many miles did Abby's dad, mom, and grandfather each drive on their trip to Niagara Falls?"

The magic bag also increases student engagement. Students get excited for their item to be chosen (everyone's item should be selected at some point); get a chance to talk about themselves; learn more about their classmates; build their background knowledge; and have a visual to attach to the number talk, making it more likely they can access the learning from the number talk and apply it later when they practice the skill on their own.

Dad Jokes

Have you heard the latest statistics? Shockingly, five out of four people admit they are bad at fractions! (The crowd snickers and groans.) Witty one-liners like this, commonly referred to as "dad jokes," are more than just cheesy digressions. They are proven to decrease stress and increase perspective-taking (Mitchell, 2019). Humor, in and of itself, is one way students (and adults) can choose to self-regulate their emotions (e.g., watching a funny video in response to feeling agitated or sad may help elevate mood and prevent undesirable actions). Engaging in collective emotions (in this case, fake laughing) produces a feeling of being part of a group, of *belonging*.

Additionally, when shared at just the right time, dad jokes can be a light-hearted jumping-off point leading to more rigorous skills or dry content.

Recently, author Bob Larkin (2020) shared "105 Dad Jokes So Bad They're Actually Hilarious." Here's how you could repurpose some of these jokes as a hook for academic content.

- **Literature:** Why is Peter Pan always flying? (*He Neverlands.*)
- **Language Arts:** Why do melons have weddings? (*Because they cantaloupe!*)
- **Science:** Did you hear about the restaurant on the moon? (*Great food, no atmosphere!*)
- **Math:** Last night I had a dream that I weighed less than a thousandth of a gram. (*I was like, 0mg.*)
- **Social Studies:** What rock group has four men that don't sing? (*Mount Rushmore.*)
- **French:** A cheese factory exploded in France. (*Da brie is everywhere!*)
- **Music:** What concert costs just 45 cents? (*50 Cent featuring Nickelback!*)
- **Art:** How does a penguin build its house? (*Igloos it together!*)
- **PE:** Why couldn't the bicycle stand up by itself? (*It was two tired.*)

Expand the Walls of Your Classroom

Perhaps one of the best ways to cultivate empathy in our students is to grant them opportunities to learn from people outside their classroom—either experts in a field or people who have experienced something firsthand (like the example about prosthetic limbs in Chapter 4). My favorite example of this practice and how it can increase academic skill and empathic capacity (for both students and their real-world partners) is the Speaking Exchange Project (FCB Brasil, 2014). The project uses videoconferencing to help the students at the CNA Language School in Brazil learn English by connecting them with seniors living in retirement homes in the United States. (Learn more at www.youtube .com/watch?v=-S-5EfwpFOk.)

The student–senior citizen partnership supplements fluency practice in the classroom with an opportunity for students to engage deep learning using spaced practice (application versus recall). Moreover, the relationships give students the chance to learn from a primary source about elders and about a culture and customs outside Brazil. Likewise, the seniors have an opportunity to meet and learn about a younger generation from another country with different customs. They even learn a little bit of Portuguese.

It's so easy to dismiss others on a journey to learn a second language when you don't know the people or their stories, but when you see someone and then build a relationship with them while working toward a joint goal, it helps break down the us-versus-them paradigm and turns "othering" into "other humans."

Try This: Design an activity or assessment that allows students to contribute content that's of interest to them or create an opportunity for students to authentically learn from a person outside your school who has experience with the skills or content being learned.

Tell one of the dad jokes listed here or one of your own to engage in collective *cheese* and hook students for more learning.

Read and Reflect

Connection can also be made within the walls of the classroom, through creative forms of assessment with teacher clarity on the learning intentions. Read the following vignette from Enrique Castro, an instructional coach in North Shore School District 112, in Highland Park, Illinois, as he describes how to connect with students through instruction and assessment. Recall your own time as a student. What learning opportunities did you connect with the most? What learning opportunities did you connect with the least? Why?

How Assessments Forge Connections with Students

By Enrique Castro

I'm confident any experienced teacher would agree with me when I say that we need to establish relationships before we begin teaching. That social-emotional component is a teacher's key to begin motivating and inspiring students' growth. For as long as I've worked with children, I've always made an effort to know them on a one-on-one basis. This promotes trust and a sense of belonging in the learning environment, leading to greater academic gains for students.

During my time as an instructional coach, I've had the opportunity to work in many different classrooms with many different teachers. Every classroom—regardless of grade level, teacher experience, content area—has one commonality: students. Each one of those students comes to school with a story. Of course, some stories are happier to hear than others, and some students are more willing to share their stories than others. As an educator, however, it is imperative you spend time attempting to learn all of your students' stories.

As an instructional coach, I once worked with a teacher who initially sought my partnership regarding the curriculum; she reported that her students were often quiet in class and their effort level was not very high. During my initial visit to her classroom, I observed that students were struggling to keep their attention on the content, and some were even disruptive and disrespectful. In my conversation with her afterward, she mentioned that she was experiencing a hard time getting through to them. I prompted her with questions that opened her eyes to the reality that she and her students were just not connecting.

My questions all centered on what was best for her students and how she knew. When asked about what avenues she took to connect with her students, her answers were generic. The lack of substance made it clear that, while she made an effort to connect, it was merely an attempt rather than an established practice that she reflected on and assessed for its efficacy.

I explained the importance of embracing each individual child's strengths and giving them the opportunity to voice their concerns. I asked her to temporarily put aside the pacing guide and textbook and listen to the stories of her students.

To elicit her students' stories, the teacher implemented dialogue journals, a practice that I had used successfully with English language learners. Dialogue journals serve as both a formative assessment and a strategy that fosters student–teacher relationships. In these journals, students responded to friendly prompts. With each response, the teacher uncovered something new about her students, and the teacher was able to respond to her students with little notes or a comment during class. Through the dialogue journals, the students built a sense of trust with the teacher. We never corrected the journals for grammatical or spelling errors, but we did use the evidence from the journals to inform instruction. We used the journal entries to give us data on what areas students (individually and as a whole) were strong in (e.g., subject–verb agreement) and which areas students needed additional practice (e.g., comma use, adjective order).

This teacher was highly successful in using this strategy to increase student engagement. She learned the importance of giving her students a voice to let her know who they were. She learned the inside scoop about her classroom and what was going on within the grade level. She discovered what general activities the children were involved in after school, and she gained insight into their lives outside school. She learned that some students had responsibilities that many of us don't face until we're on our own for the first time, and she learned that some students had parents with unreasonably high expectations for their academic achievement, while other students had parents with unreasonably low expectations. Most important, the teacher learned that students were not just being lazy or choosing to be insubordinate. They needed to feel safe and supported to engage in learning with her. From this experience, the teacher's empathy grew for these students and for others in general.

Building trust through empathetic practices is key to ensuring children learn. With that trust, we can break through barriers to learning rather than force content or assignments on students. The beautiful thing is that when we are mindful of the instructional strategies we choose and the lessons we plan, we can strike a balance between instruction and connection, just like we did with the dialogue journals.

6

Empathetic Grading and Reporting Practices

Enter just about any school in the United States and you are likely to see bulletin boards covered in college logos, teachers' college pennants hanging above their classroom doors, and slogans like "college ready" and other sentiments intended to encourage students to strive to work hard so that they can reach the ultimate in academia: attending college.

And it isn't just school systems themselves that see college as important. Some parents start focusing on getting their children into college from the time they start kindergarten. Parents in the Hollywood spotlight went to illegal lengths to secure spots for their children at the finest universities.

I'll always remember the experience I had at the beginning of my consulting career while facilitating a town hall presentation for parents in a small K–8 district transitioning to standards-based grading. As with any major shift, these parents had concerns, but I underestimated just how deep those concerns ran until one angry dad stepped up to the microphone and asked, "Just how will my son get into medical school with standards-based grading?"

I asked, "Sir, how old is your son?'

"He is 8. He's in 3rd grade."

To which I replied, "I certainly understand your concern. You want the best for your child, just like I do for my children. I do not know the answer to your question, but can you tell me how the current letter grade system will factor into his medical school admission?"

In hindsight, I'm confident I could have been much more empathetic in my response to this father. I saw his perspective, and I empathized with his feelings. But I also knew that the use of letter grades is one of the least empathetic practices we revere in U.S. education. Still, even changing the traditional grading system to a more equitable approach like standards-based grading will not eliminate some additional underlying empathy and equity concerns around the whole push for "college for all."

The College Push

College initiatives make sense on paper. Why wouldn't we want all students to go to college? I am not saying that some students shouldn't go. I am saying that the playing field is so grossly uneven that cheerful school initiatives do nothing to level it.

For one, the U.S. school system is primarily founded on competitive tenets intended to identify how students compare to one another—things like traditional grades, grade point average, and class rank. Second, by not intentionally planning through an empathetic lens, you run this risk of *implicit shaming* about the idea of college being the ultimate goal. Consider the following two examples.

In the fall of 2019, an elementary school in Florida had their "College Colors Day." Students and staff participated by wearing college garb from universities of their choice. One 4th grade student didn't own any college gear but wanted to participate and support his favorite college, the University of Tennessee. So, the little boy made his own spirit wear by pinning a hand-drawn sign onto an orange t-shirt. He was super-excited about his creation until he got to school and was bullied by his classmates for his homegrown design (Klein, 2019).

This particular story had an uplifting ending. The little boy's teacher posted a heartfelt message about the experience on Facebook, which went viral. The University of Tennessee was so impressed with this little boy's spirit and ingenuity that they produced and sold thousands of T-shirts with the boy's design and donated the proceeds to an antibullying organization.

For every story with a happy ending, however, there are likely hundreds of stories to the contrary. When we talk about topics like equity and empathy, we need to be proactive rather than reactive. Proactively, we can ask questions like, "Can all students reasonably access this activity?" "What is the goal of this activity?" "Is this the best way to reach this goal?" "How can we measure the success of this activity to reach our goal?"

The same goes for how we approach the idea of higher education in K–12 academics. Recently, I was contracted by a middle school (grades 5–8) in a rural town where the students were almost entirely the third-, fourth-, or fifth-generation residents. The vast majority of the town residents historically and currently worked either in local factories or on farms. Many of the teachers also lived in the community, and they were revered for their higher education credentials because college degrees were a rarity.

One of the days I was there happened to be their weekly College Spirit Day, where students, teachers, and administrators sported their favorite college garb. The hallways were lined with pennants and posters. College fight songs played over the loudspeakers during passing periods. It was quite a festive environment.

At this school, I worked shoulder-to-shoulder with teachers, coaching them on their instructional practices. This often included observing, modeling, and coteaching lessons. That day, I began my work in a 5th grade classroom during a social studies lesson on the effects of the Industrial Revolution. In fact, the students were engaged in an assembly line simulation. The activity concluded with discussion questions like, "Which would you rather be: an unskilled factory worker, a specialized worker, or a manager?" Some students quickly concluded that being an unskilled factory worker was the least desirable position, and they made a loose connection to the need to "do well" in school and go to college to avoid being an "unskilled worker." Other students didn't contribute much to the conversation, indicating what I thought of as their tacit agreement.

Although this lesson likely helped students understand the different workers' perspectives, I walked out of the classroom with an unsettled feeling. Something just wasn't right. As I walked down the hallway to the next classroom, I realized that the lesson not only simulated factory work but also reinforced an unspoken "class" system—a system that for many of the students in the classroom was their reality. Their parents, after all, were factory workers. What message did this lesson implicitly send to these students? If you are a skilled worker, that is *good*, but if you are a factory worker, that is *bad*? Whether students consciously recognized it or not, this message was a judgment of where these students came from. And for those who came from generations of factory workers, this lesson didn't result in learning about assembly lines. It resulted in learning about a part of their identity—a *shameful* part. When it comes to students who strive to go to college but haven't had any family members who have gone through the process before or for whom it remains difficult academically or financially, the question remains: How can we ensure these students are motivated and prepared to go to college without making being college-bound our primary focus? Well, one way we can do that is to shift our grading and reporting practices to be more empathetic.

A Little Background on Grading and Reporting Practices

The *A–F* or 100-point traditional grading system has been in place since the early 20th century. This means all parents and grandparents of current K–12 students, plus a vast majority of today's teachers, experienced a traditional grading system (Westman, 2017a). This includes myself, so I am quite empathetic to the identity threat posed when we broach the topic of shifting grading and reporting practices.

"Based on the grades we received as students," I wrote in a 2017 *Education Week* blog post, "we told ourselves we were 'good' or 'bad' students. We used our grades to tell ourselves which subjects we were 'smart' in and which ones we weren't. We used our grades to compare ourselves to our peers. Our parents used our grades to compare us to their peers and their peers' children. We used our grades to determine if we were cut out for certain careers. We allowed grades to tell us many stories about who we were. For better or for worse, these stories have played a part in shaping our identities as adults" (Westman, 2017a, para. 9). However, similar to the examples I've shared thus far in this book, many of these stories are set in shame rather than empathy.

Let's back up a bit. The letter grading system became ubiquitous in the U.S. educational landscape at the beginning of the 20th century. American families shifted from working agricultural jobs to factory work, and school became compulsory for students. Schools needed an efficient method for reporting out on how students were performing. Both instruction and grading mirrored what was happening in factories, hence the term *factory model of education*. The goals were to produce quickly, produce as well or better than your colleagues, and produce an identical product. An *A* is the highest grade in school, just like *A* is the highest grade of meat. No one consulted brain and learning research or gave any consideration to whether practices were empathetic or promoted continuous learning.

Today, we have access to an abundance of research on learning, the brain, and what works and what doesn't. The traditional letter-grading and the 100-point scale fail our students and ultimately undermine the goal of getting an education: learning. Fortunately, while we can't yet change some of our system's inherent flaws, we can work within our system's parameters to approach these holdovers from the factory model of education in an empathetic manner.

Kindergarten Deadlines

In any given kindergarten classroom, the oldest child and the youngest child could have a 364-day range between them. Think of the 5-year-olds you know; even if they were born in the same month, the gap in their abilities can be significant.

In general, we are relatively cognizant and understanding of these developmental differences. Before kids start kindergarten, we celebrate every milestone as each child reaches them. Whether a child walks at 10, 12, or 15 months, we applaud them. And when a child doesn't master a skill within the range considered developmentally appropriate (in the case of walking, by 18 months), we secure interventions to diagnose and rectify whatever the underlying obstacle is (Dubinsky & Young, 2018).

Once students enter our school system, however, we expect them all to master skills at the same pace despite our awareness of the vast range of children's skills and the natural age differences. In essence, what grading does is say, "Everyone must count to 20 by Friday. If you do, you get an A. If you count to 10, you get a C. If you can't count at all, you get an F."

This seems ludicrous, but grading students by comparing their progress to others rather than assessing them on their individual growth has a cumulative effect. The Common Core State Standards (and others) are meant for students at any given grade level to master by the end of the school year. To keep with the counting example, the kindergarten standard states that by the end of the school year, students will count to 100 by ones and tens (Common Core State Standards Initiative, 2020).

But because of other flawed practices (like report cards), educators set arbitrary goalposts for students to make reporting more effective and end up grading students within these arbitrary parameters: count to 20 by Friday; count to 40 by next Friday; count to 60 by the following Friday. And we grade students each week. If a student couldn't count to 20 on the first Friday and gets an F, what is likely to happen on the subsequent Fridays? You get more examples of the students failing, which cumulatively creates both a skill and a self-confidence deficit. For those of you who teach grades 4–12 and wonder why so many students lack skills and motivation, well, herein lies the answer.

Data Are Attached to Students, Not Teachers

I often hear comments like, "We've swung too far back. We used to hold kids back, and now everyone gets a trophy at our honor roll assembly." In fact, neither of these practices is empathetic. How is it helpful for students to fail a grade and have to repeat it? Similarly, how valuable is it for us to pass kids along regardless of whether they are ready or not? In addition, giving all kids a trophy for learning even when learning does not occur is also potentially shaming. Students know when they haven't learned something. So, when we give them a trophy anyway, they can see it as a form of pity, which is a derivative of shame.

We need to stop looking at things as black or white—one end of the spectrum to the other. Instead, data should live with students and follow them from one grade level to another. With technology, at the beginning of 3rd grade, we *can* and *should* know if a student has not yet mastered a skill instructed in 2nd grade, and we can start there. The 2nd grade teacher is not the owner of the 2nd graders' data. Each student is the owner of their own data, their own story. When I say "data," I do not mean grades. I am referring to evidence of learning proficiency, which leads me to the next holdover from the factory model of education: report cards.

Report Cards

Grades and report cards are like peanut butter and jelly. We have been accustomed to think of grades and report cards as a bonded pair. But are they really? I think not. Instead, try looking at report cards as analogous to bank statements.

It is compulsory in most states that schools send official report cards home one or multiple times each school year. This is similar to how banks are mandated to send their clients formal bank statements at the end of each month. Both of these documents (report cards and bank statements) become completely obsolete the moment they are created.

Why? In the time it takes to compile and send a bank statement to a patron, that person could have made multiple withdrawals from or deposits into their account. The balance listed on the statement is no longer an accurate report of the account's current status. The frequency of change to a bank account is impossible to capture without looking at the data in real time.

This is the same phenomenon with grades on report cards. It is impossible to capture a student's learning with a single grade on a report card because, like a bank account, student learning is always changing. As students make progress toward their learning goals, their "balance" goes up. This is normal, but what report cards tend to do is create misguided pressure for teachers to cover content by arbitrary dates to satisfy the false belief that students must complete certain learning by the end of the marking period.

Before the advent of technological tools that can help all industries operate more effectively, efficiently, and accurately, schools had to send home paper report cards at designated dates within a school year to communicate students' progress. Today, however, we have other options. Just like most people can view their bank accounts in real time on a website or with an app, students, parents, and teachers can do the same thing. Technology not only makes assessing and reporting more efficient for teachers, but also removes the need for judgment (i.e., a grade) because the data give teachers, students, and their parents a clearer picture of students' progress in real time. Figures 6.1, 6.2, and 6.3 provide three visuals of how we can track students' individual and collective progress toward meeting the success criteria using a single point rubric and then aggregating data to inform small-group, targeted instruction.

Because the skills and concepts that students learn are yearlong objectives, educators can then differentiate instruction based on the specific skills and standards that students still need to master before introducing new skills and risking creating a more massive deficit. Then, you can start to look for students who fall outside the range of normal (e.g., a student who cannot count to 100 by the end of kindergarten). If, at the end of the first trimester, the student cannot count to 10 consistently as indicated by the data you have kept, this is when you bring parents into the mix. You don't wait for the report card to let parents know you are concerned (just like a bank will contact you after you are overdrawn; they don't wait for the bank statement to tell you).

By looking at the data in real time and doing what you can to make learning progress as transparent as possible for parents, you can provide appropriate interventions for students. If you ensure they master counting to 100 before you expect them to tackle the subsequent skills of adding and subtracting, you avoid potentially putting students at a serious deficit in their learning.

By taking steps to remove the judgment, competitive factor, and subjectivity of grading and reporting, you eliminate many practices that implicitly or explicitly lack empathy for the complex nature and timeline of learning.

FIGURE 6.1
Using Single-Point Rubrics to Track Student Progress

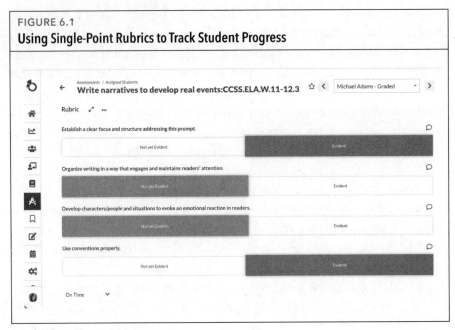

Source: Created at www.otus.com.

FIGURE 6.2
Tracking Students' Progress Over Time

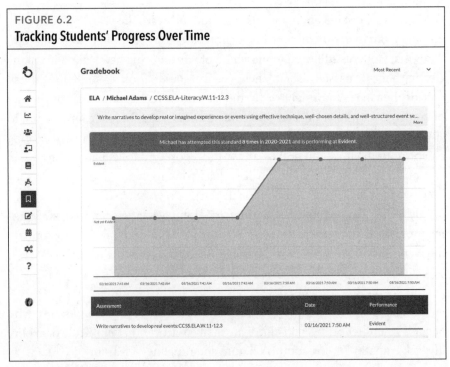

Source: Created at www.otus.com.

FIGURE 6.3
Using Data to Form Flexible Groups

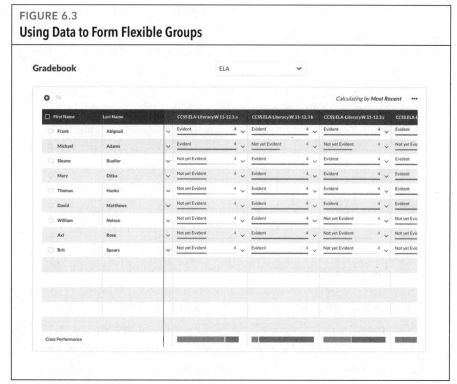

Source: Created at www.otus.com.

Mixing Behavior and Academic Performance

All of the grading considerations discussed here presuppose that student progress is reported purely based on academic indicators and not behavioral.

Grades historically have been used as both a motivator and a punishment. Although research shows that incentivizing achievement (receiving high grades) results in some motivational gain, no research shows that receiving low grades results in increased student motivation. "More often, low grades lead students to withdraw from learning," according to Thomas Guskey (2015). "To protect self-images, many students regard the low grade as irrelevant or meaningless. Others may blame themselves for the low grade but feel helpless to improve" (p. 98).

Aside from not motivating students, lowering an academic grade to punish an undesirable behavior diminishes the integrity of the grade itself and again seeks to shame rather than empathize with the root of the behavior.

"Undesirable behaviors" are somewhat subjective because educators (as well as parents and other adults) have different triggers, tolerance levels, and reactions to actions by their students. What may be a big deal to some teachers may be irrelevant to others. This inconsistency, in and of itself, can be unsettling and dysregulating to some students, causing an increase in undesirable behaviors (as discussed in detail in Chapter 3).

With regard to grading practices, you must separate academic progress and student skill (or "soft skills"). You don't need to choose one or the other; instead, you should report on both as separate entities, using the same method you use to assess academics: set clear learning intentions and success criteria for meeting these intentions. Then, report on progress toward the learning goals.

It is crucial to create both grading practices and the corresponding learning intentions and success criteria for student skills with input from teacher representatives and to assess them with the same success criteria. As an example, the staff members at Honowai Elementary School in Waipahu, Hawaii, collaborated to determine their school's nonnegotiable grading principles through a series of professional learning sessions and staff compromises (see Figure 6.4) (influenced by the work of Ken O'Connor in his 2010 book *A Repair Kit for Grading*). Some principles took a bit of negotiating, and others were never adopted. The 13 principles that made the cut are adhered to by all staff members to provide students with clear and consistent expectations.

At a middle school in the San Francisco Bay Area, the teachers and administrators worked together to clearly define and create a shared understanding of student skills. They then created the rubric shown in Figure 6.5 (similar to the academic rubrics teachers and students used) to clearly list the learning intentions and success criteria for those student skills to allow teachers and students to track their behaviors more objectively and routinely.

In summary, grading and reporting practices in the United States are rooted in long-standing traditions of comparing, conflating, and confusing what constitutes both academic and social-emotional learning. Through the lens of empathy and a keen focus on the goal of learning and growing for all students, shifting from historically accepted grading and reporting practices to more empathetic approaches becomes less of an overwhelming undertaking and more of a nonnegotiable part of our educational infrastructure to guarantee success.

FIGURE 6.4
Principles of Standards-Based Grading

At Honowai Elementary School we believe
Student behaviors should not be factored into academic "grades."
Late assignments should not be penalized academically.
"Extra credit" or bonus points should not be offered to increase a student's grade.
When working in groups, a student should be graded on his or her performance, not as a group.
Evidence from formative assessments should inform instruction and not be averaged into a grade.
The grade book should be organized by standards and learning goals, rather than by assignment.
Clear descriptions of achievement expectations should be given to students.
Grades are based on performance aligned to standards and learning goals rather than assignment.
Zeros aren't used for missing evidence. Alternatives (ex. "insufficient evidence") are used instead.
Habits of scholarship (student skills) should be assessed and reported separately.
Grades should be for communication, not motivation or punishment.
Students are part of the grading process via goal-setting, choice, and tracking their progress toward mastery.
Teachers ensure that students are encouraged to honestly report their progress and advocate for themselves by creating conducive learning environments.

Source: Adapted by Lisa Westman for Honowai Elementary School from *A repair kit for grading: 15 fixes for broken grades* (2nd ed.), 2010, by K. O'Connor. Boston, MA: Pearson. Used with permission.

Reflect: What traditions or initiatives can your school revamp to proactively consider all students' life experiences and circumstances? How can you include students in the process to better reach the initiatives' goals?

FIGURE 6.5
Student Skills That Support Learning

Demonstrate effective work habits	❏ I know what my learning goal is. ❏ I know what I need to do to reach my goal. ❏ I worked toward my learning goal today. What I did: _____ ❏ I sought feedback from my teacher. What my teacher said: _____
Come prepared to learn	❏ My Chromebook was charged and ready. ❏ I had my materials. ❏ I followed the dress code. ❏ I followed the technology agreement.
Collaborate with others appropriately and productively	❏ I knew who my partner(s) were. ❏ I used positive, respectful, encouraging vocabulary with my partner(s). ❏ I sought my partner's input by asking questions. ❏ I listened to my partner. ❏ My partner and I made a work plan. (attach here)
Demonstrate self-management/ regulation	❏ I showed persistence today. How so? _____ ❏ I paid attention to detail in my work. How so? _____

 Try This: Consider taking some small steps toward more empathetic grading practices; choose one strategy to start:

1. Separate student skills from academics. Don't reward or punish students with grades.

2. Award an *A* for "meets all success criteria."

3. Use a single-point rubric with learning intentions and success criteria to help students track their progress toward mastery.

Read and Reflect

Read this vignette from Cathy Fisher, the director of teaching and learning in Maercker School District 60, in Westmont, Illinois, as she discusses leading a change in grading and reporting practices and how to do that empathetically. How does her journey compare and contrast to change initiatives you have led or been a part of in your education career?

Our Journey Toward More Empathic Grading and Reporting
By Cathy Fisher

In education, because the time to learn and prepare together is limited, we too often move forward with instructional changes or implementation without providing the time needed to build shared understanding and the capacity for independent implementation. Input from administrators and teacher leaders drove the pace District 60 set to address grading and reporting practices. Our next steps were continually determined and adjusted in real time, based on the circumstances at the time.

Richly diverse District 60 serves approximately 1,450 students in preschool through 8th grade. Twenty-one percent of our students qualify for English learner services, and 35 percent qualify for free or reduced-price lunch. Providing a systematic approach to ensure a caring, participatory, and equitable learning environment is a priority for our district. The district's continuous improvement plan is guided by the Consortium for Educational Change's (CEC) Continuous Improvement Framework. The framework is designed around three critical areas: Focus on Learning, Focus on Collaboration, and Focus on Results. Each school participated in a System Assessment visit, where a group of visiting educators—through document review and interviews with staff, parents, and students—provided feedback and identified opportunities for improvement, based on the framework. The feedback identified grading and reporting practices as an opportunity for improvement, and based on the Focus on Learning continuum, clarifying and communicating the curriculum was our starting point.

> Clarifying and Communicating the Curriculum: We ensure that every teacher can assist all students and their families in knowing the essential learning outcomes so that they can help in monitoring performance in relation to these outcomes.

Our goals for this work were:

- Understand prioritized standards, learning intentions, and success criteria.
- Prioritize the standards and develop learning intentions and success criteria.
- Develop formative assessments aligned to the success criteria to monitor growth.
- Implement instructional change through the use of formative assessments to drive differentiation.
- Implement grading and reporting procedures that provide real-time data related to a student's progress toward mastery of the success criteria.

The success of this implementation was extremely important to us, and just like we want teachers to empathize with their students, we, as leaders, also make it a priority to empathize with our teachers and parents. To ensure a successful roll-out, we decided to "go slow to go fast." The Administrative Leadership Team spent six months focused on professional learning to understand the why and how of priority standards, learning intentions, and success criteria, before we made this an initiative for teachers. Effective instructional change requires the leadership of the school administration. Because we took the time to build a shared understanding, we were also able to develop a timeline to complete this work that didn't overwhelm the system and allowed flexibility in the pace of prioritizing standards and identifying learning intentions and success criteria.

To make sure our perception of "not overwhelming the system" was aligned with what teachers view, we provided an overview of the process to Building Leadership Team members at all three schools. We felt providing this foundation was important so that all teacher leaders were informed, even though their school or content area might not engage with the work until a later date. Kindergarten through 5th grade mathematics was in the third year of implementing new curriculum resources, and English language arts (ELA) was in the first year, so the district began the process of prioritizing the standards with the K–5 math teacher leaders. This prioritization requires significant vertical articulation, so working with small groups of teacher leaders is an efficient approach. As the teacher leaders identified learning intentions and success criteria, we learned to consider which skills and concepts students could master and which ones teachers would need to monitor for growth. These rich, student-centered discussions were crucial for building a shared understanding that resulted in sound decision making rooted in an empathetic connection with our students' and one another's perspectives.

After the K–5 math teachers completed their first draft of priority standards, learning intentions, and success criteria, the group moved on to align their formative assessments with the success criteria. Our teachers have spent countless hours developing unit plans and pacing guides to ensure continuity of instruction. The priority standards, learning intentions, and success criteria did not negate that work but instead provided the clarity needed to ensure teachers, students, and parents know the essential learning outcomes and can monitor their progress. Certainly, we maintained, repurposed, and eliminated some learning activities and assessments, but the grade-level teams made those decisions through the lens of the learning intentions and success criteria that teacher leaders developed, not the pacing guide provided by the publisher. We took careful measures to ensure we were respecting our teachers' expertise and preserving their autonomy.

The district used the model that K–5 math teachers created to begin prioritizing the standards and identifying learning intentions and success criteria with the K–5 ELA teacher leaders. Over time, we continued to leverage our internal capacity to bolster that of other departments.

All of this foundational work is essential to create equitable grading and reporting practices. Without clarity of learning intentions and success criteria, grading and reporting remain inconsistent and sometimes arbitrary. The district's grading and reporting system includes priority standards and learning intentions written in parent- and student-friendly language. It also allows students to have multiple opportunities and methods to demonstrate mastery of the success criteria. Every learning intention has a single-point rubric based on the success criteria. Teachers use the same single-point rubric for every formative assessment, whether done through teacher observation, an exit slip, a quiz, or an assignment. Teachers indicate whether the success criteria are evident or not evident and record this data into the grade book so that teachers, students, and parents can see student progress toward mastery of the learning intention. This data collection drives differentiation, focuses on small-group instruction, and informs students of their practice and growth opportunities.

Clarifying and communicating the curriculum through priority standards, learning intentions, and success criteria provides transparency for students and parents, which we hope demonstrates our understanding of these stakeholder groups' needs. When we report whether the success criteria are evident or not, students and parents can monitor student progress, and teachers can provide students with targeted instruction. This shift is not about grading and reporting but about differentiating instructional practice and being empathetic to students' individual paths and processes to ensure learning occurs. Shifting instructional practice can be difficult for all parties involved. It is essential to be mindful of what is happening within the system, including teachers' feelings, and develop a realistic implementation plan.

When I partnered with Maercker School District 60 as they worked to reform grading and reporting practices, I was able to witness firsthand how empathetic leadership practices beget empathic teaching practices (see the example of using artistic expressions in Chapter 4). I also recognize that as a teacher reading this book, you may feel that you aren't in control of the leadership styles of your organization. Perhaps you feel that your leadership doesn't yet exemplify empathy. This is a tricky situation, of course, and one I like to look at from our own locus of control and reflect on how we can strengthen our own empathetic skill to better understand our leaders' perspectives and empathize with our organizations' needs.

Recommended Readings

A topic this multifaceted deserves careful and extensive research before implementing changes to ensure they are the right choices for you. What I provide are
compelling arguments to commit to such shifts. If you are interested in doing a
deep dive into grading and reporting practices, I highly recommend these books:

Guskey, T. R. (2015). *On your mark: Challenging the conventions of grading and reporting.*
    Bloomington, IN: Solution Tree Press.
Guskey, T. R., & Brookhart, S. M. (Eds.). (2019). *What we know about grading: What
    works, what doesn't, and what's next.* Alexandria, VA: ASCD.
O'Connor, K. (2010). *A repair kit for grading: 15 fixes for broken grades* (2nd ed.). Boston:
    Pearson.

7

Where Do You Go from Here? Actionable Steps to Become a More Empathetic Educator

Thank you for sticking with me until the end of this book. Now, let's take a moment to look back so that you can move forward. At this point, I hope you have expanded your understanding of the three types of empathy—affective, cognitive, and behavioral—and contemplated the role empathy plays in our schools during lesson planning, instruction, assessment, programming, and discipline and how it affects the mental health of our students and ourselves. In Chapter 1, you completed an empathy assessment and an empathy self-reflection (see p. 2). Retake these now and reflect. Have you grown? About what areas are you most interested in learning more? What questions do you have?

Perhaps you are wondering where you go next. You may feel inspired to make lots of changes, or you may feel overwhelmed and don't want to do anything. Either way, my advice to you is the same: start small and take one step at a time. This chapter will outline a process to take your first steps and provide you with some tools to help you along the way.

Even though empathy is a skill that we are born with and develop starting in our first days and months of life, similar to how we build speech, you can learn and strengthen empathy in adulthood. Current research from Harvard, Yale, Stanford, the National University of Singapore, and A*STAR (also in Singapore) on building empathy indicates that an individual's motivation for increasing their empathic skill is directly correlated to their success in growing their empathy (Weisz, Ong, Carlson, & Zaki, 2020). The great thing about growing skills is that there is no ceiling; so, no matter where you currently fall on the spectrum of empathy, the process outlined here will result in continued growth.

Please note that any change worth making will be challenging at times. This is how you know the change is occurring. Stick with it, and you will be victorious. I strongly encourage you to partner with an instructional coach or trusted colleague and go through this process together.

Step 1: Identify Your Motivation

In life, we set a lot of goals. Sometimes, we set goals without reflecting on the *why*. This often happens in a professional setting, where, at some arbitrary time, we are told to set a goal, so we do so out of compliance rather than organic desire. Therefore, before you set any goals concerning empathy, let's take the time to reflect on our individual motivations. Use the chart in Figure 7.1 to help you determine your personal motivation for wanting to increase your empathic capacity. As you go through this process, remember that reasons are personal. Whatever your motivation is, it is valid, so try to refrain from judging your own thoughts (in other words, demonstrate empathy for yourself first).

Step 2: Set Your First Goal

Now that you have had some time to reflect on your motivations, you can set your first goal. Even if this book was assigned reading and you are still not sold on this idea, I encourage you to try setting one goal to see if this sparks anything in you.

Your motivation drives your goal. What is your primary motivation? Do you want your students to feel connected? Do you want to go home and feel connected to others and look forward to the next day? Do you want your students' achievement to increase? Your goal is personal. Whatever your goal is, that will drive your action plan. The best way to reach a large goal is to set a series of smaller goals.

For example, if your primary desired outcome were to become healthier, the smaller goals along the way might be (1) increase fruit and vegetable intake, (2) decrease processed foods, and (3) increase physical activity. Mastering these things one at a time is more realistic than trying to master all of them at the same time.

A series of smaller accomplishments will increase your self-efficacy, which in turn increases the likelihood you will remain committed to your primary

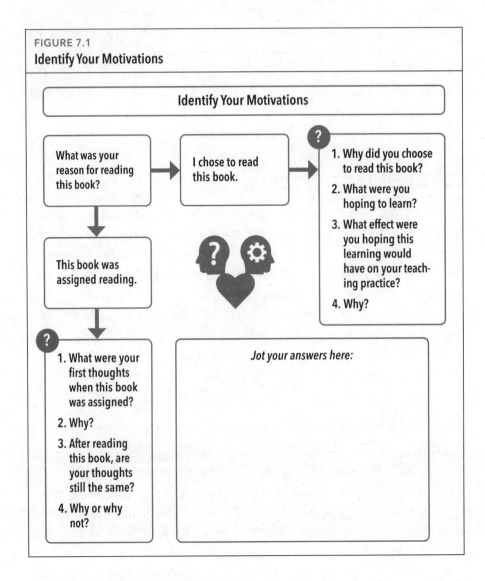

FIGURE 7.1
Identify Your Motivations

goal and increase the sustainability of the changes you make. The same princi-
ple applies to setting your empathy goals. You are autonomous in the number
of goals you set and the pace at which you go. Remember, it is not a race or a
competition; as you meet one goal, set another.

First, start with your end goal, your motivation. This is your "I want" statement. Some common motivations:

- I want my students to feel safer.
- I want my students to learn more.
- I want to feel more connected to my students.

From this primary goal, set your first, smaller goal. This is your "I will" statement. Some examples of smaller goals related to those above:

- I will ensure all of my students belong to our learning community.
- I will ensure my curriculum is inclusive for my students.
- I will incorporate instructional strategies that are both effective and responsive to my students' academic and social-emotional needs.

 Reflect: What is your motivation? What is your first goal?

Step 3: Determine Your Success Criteria and Take Baseline Data

Now that you have your goal, let's determine how you will know when you have met your goal. The most essential determiner of whether or not a goal will be met is having a clear idea of what success looks like—that is, having success criteria. Decide the success criteria for meeting your goal before making any changes. This way, you will be able to assess your progress along the way.

Answer the following questions to help you determine your success criteria. Remember that if at any point this process becomes overwhelming, seek the partnership of an instructional coach or trusted colleague who can assist in asking you these questions.

1. What does this behavior (e.g., *student belonging, curriculum, instruction*) currently look like in your classroom?
2. What will look different in your classroom when you meet your goal (e.g., *all students feel they belong, the curriculum is inclusive, instruction is more responsive*)?

Your responses to the second question are your success criteria. These are personal to you and inform the strategies you choose to use (more on this in Step 4). Some examples of success criteria:

Goal: All students will feel they belong.
Possible Success Criteria: Students participate in class; students advocate for themselves; students encourage one another; students make connections between the content and their lives.
Note: The Project for Education Research That Scales (PERTS) offers excellent courses and checklists with success criteria for student belonging, student voice, and so on: www.perts.net/elevate.

Goal: Design and use a more inclusive curriculum.
Possible Success Criteria: Students are more willing to share their personal stories; students ask one another more questions; students complete more work.

Goal: Use more responsive instructional strategies.
Possible Success Criteria: Students are more engaged in class; students complete more work; students' academic achievement increases.

Now that you have your success criteria, take some baseline data on what your current goal looks like in your classroom. For example, perhaps your goal is to see an increase in student engagement and participation. Your success criteria include seeing an increase in the number of questions students ask you and their classmates and an increase in the number of connections students make between the content and their lives. Take some baseline data (a simple tally of the number of connections made is all that's necessary) and then set a realistic goal. This goal is somewhat arbitrary, so set the goal based on your current class makeup and comfort level trying new strategies. See Figure 7.2 for an example using the goal of increasing engagement.

Step 4: Choose Strategies and Use Checklists

Dr. Atul Gawande, acclaimed surgeon, speaker, and author of *The Checklist Manifesto*, gives empirical evidence in his book that the use of checklists helps us perform with greater precision and ultimate success. Whether you are a doctor, a teacher, or a pilot, a quality checklist is invaluable in ensuring you meet our goals, and you meet them the right way (Gawande, 2014).

Throughout this book, I have outlined a variety of effective instructional strategies that will result in more empathetic learning environments. To meet your goal, choose a strategy that you would like to try implementing and create your own checklist, using this book as a guide or coming up with your own steps. Talk to your partner and use the checklist to guide your implementation and next steps.

Step 5: Monitor Growth

As you strive to implement your chosen strategy, remember these two clichés: Rome wasn't built in a day, and practice makes perfect. Give yourself time and

---

FIGURE 7.2

Data Collection and Goal-Setting Tool

Goal: Increase Virtual Class Participation and Engagement

Student Name	Participation Type (check all/each that apply)	
Tomasita	❏❏❏ Responded Aloud	❏❏❏ Asked Question
	❏❏❏ Responded in Chat	❏❏❏ Answered Question
	❏❏❏ Made/Shared Personal Connection	❏❏❏ Other (identify):
Jamarion	❏❏❏ Responded Aloud	❏❏❏ Asked Question
	❏❏❏ Responded in Chat	❏❏❏ Answered Question
	❏❏❏ Made/Shared Personal Connection	❏❏❏ Other (identify):
Darci	❏❏❏ Responded Aloud	❏❏❏ Asked Question
	❏❏❏ Responded in Chat	❏❏❏ Answered Question
	❏❏❏ Made/Shared Personal Connection	❏❏❏ Other (identify):
Solomon	❏❏❏ Responded Aloud	❏❏❏ Asked Question
	❏❏❏ Responded in Chat	❏❏❏ Answered Question
	❏❏❏ Made/Shared Personal Connection	❏❏❏ Other (identify):
Minnie	❏❏❏ Responded Aloud	❏❏❏ Asked Question
	❏❏❏ Responded in Chat	❏❏❏ Answered Question
	❏❏❏ Made/Shared Personal Connection	❏❏❏ Other (identify):

Tally of Student Participation

_____ # of students who participated once

_____ # of students who participated more than once

_____ # of students who did not participate at all

Tally of Total Response Types:

____ Responded Aloud

____ Responded in Chat

____ Made/Shared Personal Connection

____ Asked Question

____ Answered Question

GOAL

Increase student participation to 90 percent of students participating at least once in a 45-minute class period.

Increase student participation to at least 70 percent of students participating more than once in a 45-minute class period.

treat yourself with grace as you work to develop a more empathetic teaching practice. Determine a check-in time commensurate with your goal and corresponding strategy (e.g., every Monday, every other Thursday, the first of the month) to collect the same data using the same collection tool you used to collect your baseline data. Then, analyze your growth.

Have you met your goal? If so, do you want more time to practice this strategy, or are you ready to set your next goal? Are you approaching your goal? If so, is the progress you have made satisfactory with you? If so, keep going. If your progress is not as robust as you would like, contemplate choosing a different strategy (in addition to or instead of your initial strategy) to meet your goal. Your instructional coach or trusted colleague can be another set of eyes and ears in your classroom. This person may see things you are overlooking in your implementation or have other helpful feedback for you.

Celebrate

No matter where you are in your journey, celebrate your reflectiveness, open-mindedness, and dedication to the field of education just by completing this book. And, as you continue on your journey to create a more empathetic learning environment for your students, celebrate your small victories along the way. We are all ever-changing beings with rich stories full of successes and failures. Sometimes the biggest obstacle in our way is ourselves. If you feel yourself slipping, check in with yourself, and always remember to empathize with yourself first.

At times, you will still question the best way to empathize with your students, your colleagues, and yourself. In those times when clarity evades you, never underestimate the power of a genuine smile. Smile with your mouth and through your eyes, and your empathy will shine through, too. I am cheering you on from here and would love to hear about your successes. You can always find me on Twitter @lisa_westman and share away.

References

Anderson, M. (2018, September). Getting consistent with consequences. *Educational Leadership, 76(1)* 26–33.

Brackett, M. (2019). *Permission to feel: Unlocking the power of emotions to help our kids, ourselves, and our society thrive.* New York: Celadon Books.

Brown, B. (2007). *I thought it was just me (But it isn't).* New York: Gotham.

Brown, P. C., McDaniel, M. A., & Roediger III, H. (2018). *Make it stick: The science of successful learning.* Cambridge, MA: Belknap Harvard.

Burnham, K. (2020, August 25). Culturally responsive teaching: 5 strategies for educators [blog post]. Retrieved September 29, 2020 from *Northeastern University Graduate Programs*, at https://www.northeastern.edu/graduate/blog/culturally -responsive-teaching-strategies/

Center on the Developing Child at Harvard University. (2017). *Three principles to improve outcomes for children and families.* Retrieved March 5, 2021, from https://developing child.harvard.edu/resources/three-early-childhood-development-principles -improve-child-family-outcomes/

Centers for Disease Control and Prevention. (2020, March 25). *Data & statistics on autism spectrum disorder.* Retrieved August 25, 2020, from https://www.cdc.gov /ncbddd/autism/data.html

Cocca-Leffler, M. (2019). *Same way Ben.* Chicago: Albert Whitman.

Common Core State Standards Initiative. (2020). *Kindergarten: Counting & cardinality.* Retrieved May 07, 2020, from http://www.corestandards.org/Math/Content/K/CC/

DiAngelo, R. (2018). *White fragility: Why it's so hard for white people to talk about racism.* Boston: Beacon Press.

Dubinsky, D., & Young, P. (2018). Baby milestone: Walking [online article]. Retrieved May 7, 2020, from *BabyCenter* at https://www.babycenter.com/0_baby-milestone -walking_6507.bc

Ducharme. (2019, June 20). Suicide rates are the highest they've been since WWII. *Time.* Retrieved April 30, 2020, from https://time.com/5609124/us-suicide-rate-increase/

Facing History and Ourselves. (n.d.). Identity charts. Retrieved September 30, 2020, from https://www.facinghistory.org/resource-library/teaching-strategies/identity -charts

FCB Brasil. (2014, May 7). CNA-Speaking Exchange [YouTube video]. Retrieved September 23, 2020, from https://www.youtube.com/watch?v=-S-5EfwpFOk

Frey, N., Fisher, D., & Smith, D. (2019). *All learning is social and emotional: Helping students develop essential skills for the classroom and beyond.* Alexandria, VA: ASCD.

Gabriel, A., Harper, K., Steed, H., & Temkin, D. (2019). State laws promoting social, emotional, and academic development leave room for improvement [blog post]. Retrieved March 5, 2021, from *Child Trends* at https://www.childtrends.org/blog/state-laws -promoting-social-emotional-and-academic-development-leave-room-for-improvement

Gawande, A. (2014). *The checklist manifesto: How to get things right.* Gurgaon, India: Penguin Random House.

Gladwell, M. (Host). (2019a, June 20). Puzzle Rush [Audio podcast episode]. In *Revisionist History.* Panoply Media. http://revisionisthistory.com/episodes /31-puzzle-rush.

Gladwell, M. (Host). (2019b, June 27). The Tortoise and the Hare [Audio podcast episode]. In *Revisionist History.* Panoply Media. http://revisionisthistory.com /episodes/32-the-tortoise-and-the-hare

Gonzalez, J. (2016, September 24). How pineapple charts revolutionize professional development [blog post]. Retrieved December 3, 2020, from *Cult of Pedagogy* at https://www.cultofpedagogy.com/pineapple-charts/

Guskey, T. R. (2015). *On your mark: Challenging the conventions of grading and reporting.* Bloomington, IN: Solution Tree Press.

Guskey, T. R., & Brookhart, S. M. (Eds.). (2019). *What we know about grading: What works, what doesn't, and what's next.* Alexandria, VA: ASCD.

Hattie, J. (2012). *Visible learning for teachers & students: Maximizing impact on learning.* New York: Routledge.

Hoerr, T. R. (2017). *The formative five: Fostering grit, empathy, and other success skills every student needs.* Alexandria, VA: ASCD.

IDRA. (2020, April 29). *Six goals of educational equity.* Retrieved December 3, 2020, from https://www.idra.org/equity-assistance-center/six-goals-of-education-equity/

Jennings, P. A., & Siegel, D. J. (2019). *The trauma-sensitive classroom: Building resilience with compassionate teaching.* New York: W.W. Norton.

Kagan, S., & Kagan, M. (2017). *Kagan cooperative learning.* San Clemente, CA: Kagan Publishing.

Khoury, L., Tang, Y. L., Bradley, B., Cubells, J. F., & Ressler, K. J. (2010, December). Substance use, childhood traumatic experience, and post-traumatic stress disorder in an urban civilian population. *Depression and Anxiety.* Retrieved August 26, 2020, from https://www.ncbi.nlm.nih.gov/pmc/articles/PMC3051362/

Klein, A. (2019, September 9). A kid was teased for his homemade University of Tennessee logo. Then UT made his drawing into a real shirt. *Washington Post.* Retrieved May 4, 2020, from https://www.washingtonpost.com/lifestyle /2019/09/09/fourth-grader-was-teased-his-homemade-university-tennessee -logo-then-ut-made-his-drawing-into-real-shirt

Korbey, H. (2020, July 28). Is it time to drop "finding the main idea" and teach reading in a new way? [blog post] Retrieved March 5, 2021, from *Edutopia* at https://www .edutopia.org/article/it-time-drop-finding-main-idea-and-teach-reading-new-way

Larkin, B. (2020). 105 dad jokes so bad they're actually hilarious [blog post]. Retrieved March 5, 2021, from *Best Life Online* at https://bestlifeonline.com /dad-jokes-so-bad-theyre-actually-hilarious/

Many, T. W., & Horrell, T. (2014, January). Prioritizing the standards using R.E.A.L. criteria. *TEPSA News, 71*(1), 1–2.

Marsh, J. (2012). Do mirror neurons give us empathy? *Greater Good Magazine.* Retrieved July 2, 2020, from https://greatergood.berkeley.edu/article/item/do_mirror_neurons_give_empathy

Minahan, J., & Rappaport, N. (2013). *The behavior code: A practical guide to understanding and teaching the most challenging students.* Cambridge, MA: Harvard Education Press.

Mitchell, H. (2019, February 27). What can science tell us about dad jokes? *Wall Street Journal.* Retrieved September 23, 2020, from https://www.wsj.com/articles/what-can-science-tell-us-about-dad-jokes-11551278885

O'Connor, K. (2010). *A repair kit for grading: 15 fixes for broken grades* (2nd ed.). Boston: Pearson.

Psychology Today. (2020). Identity. Retrieved December 3, 2020, from https://www.psychologytoday.com/us/basics/identity

Quaglia Institute for School Voice and Aspirations. (2016). *Student voice report.* Thousand Oaks, CA: Corwin Press.

Rasmussen, P. R. (2010). *Quest to feel good.* New York: Routledge.

Riess, H., (with Neporent, L.). (2018). *Empathy effect: Seven neuroscience-based keys for transforming the way we live, love, work, and connect across differences.* Boulder, CO: Sounds True.

SAMHSA. (2020, April 29). Understanding child trauma. Retrieved March 11, 2021, from https://www.samhsa.gov/child-trauma/understanding-child-trauma

Singer, T. W. (2015). Get explicit about implicit bias [blog post]. Retrieved March 5, 2021, from *Tonya Ward Singer: Courageous Learning* at https://tonyasinger.com/get-explicit-about-implicit-bias/

Southern Methodist University. (2018, June 12). Higher empathy people process music differently in the brain. *Neuroscience News.* Retrieved March 1, 2021, from https://neurosciencenews.com/empathy-music-processing-9313/

Szalavitz, M., & Perry, B. D. (2010). *Born for love: Why empathy is essential—and endangered.* New York: HarperPaperbacks.

Thiers, N. (2017, June). Making progress possible: A conversation with Michael Fullan. *Educational Leadership, 74.* Retrieved March 11, 2021, from http://www.ascd.org/publications/educational-leadership/jun17/vol74/num09/Making-Progress-Possible@-A-Conversation-with-Michael-Fullan.aspx

Thompson. (2011, September 30). Is nonverbal communication a numbers game? [blog post]. Retrieved July 2, 2020, from *Beyond Words* at https://www.psychologytoday.com/us/blog/beyond-words/201109/is-nonverbal-communication-numbers-game

Tomlinson, C. A. (2021). *So each may soar: The principles and practices of learner-centered classrooms.* Alexandria, VA: ASCD.

Tull, M. (2020, April 19). The interesting relationship between PTSD and shame [online article]. Retrieved June 21, 2020, from *Verywell Mind* at https://www.verywellmind.com/ptsd-and-shame-2797529

Uptas, A. (2018). This artist combines photos from different parts of the world to show the contrast between them [online article]. Retrieved March 5, 2021, from *DeMilked* at https://www.demilked.com/contrast-between-worlds-ugur-gallen/

Weisz, E., Ong, D. C., Carlson, R. W., & Zaki, J. (2020, November 19). Building empathy through motivation-based interventions [online article]. *Emotion*. Retrieved March 5, 2021, from https://doi.org/10.1037/emo0000929

Westman, L. (2017a, March 14). Standards-based grading made my kid average [blog post]. Retrieved March 5, 2021, from *Education Week* at https://www.edweek.org /education/opinion-standards-based-grading-made-my-kid-average/2017/03

Westman, L. (2017b, August 31). The greatest deficiency in education is our obsession with showcasing deficits [blog post]. Retrieved March 5, 2021, from *Put Me in Coach* at https://lisawestmanblog.wordpress.com

Westman, L. (2018). *Student-driven differentiation: 8 steps to harmonize learning in the classroom*. Thousand Oaks, CA: Corwin.

Winfrey, O. (2011, October 19). The powerful lesson Maya Angelou taught Oprah [video]. Retrieved March 5, 2021, from https://www.oprah.com/oprahs-lifeclass /the-powerful-lesson-maya-angelou-taught-oprah-video

Zaki, J. (2019). *The war for kindness: Building empathy in a fractured world*. New York: Crown.

Index

The letter *f* following a page locator denotes a figure.

affective empathy, 3–4, 44
altruism born of suffering, 30
art, increasing perspective taking with, 56–59
assessment. *See also* grading and reporting
  practices
    connecting with students through, 84–86
    formative, 69–71
    time element in, 77–79
Autism Spectrum Disorder (ASD), 23

behavior
    eliminating trauma triggers to change,
      24–25
    lowering grades to punish, 96
    mixing academic performance and, 95
    motivations for, 25–26, 28, 29
    redirecting, 31, 33, 37
    teacher inconsistency, effect on, 96
behavioral empathy, 4–5, 44, 59–61
being real in relationship building, 30–31
belonging
    cultivating by building relationships, 29–32
    importance of, 10
Black Lives Matter movement, 9

celebrate becoming an empathetic educator, 110
checklists, for becoming an empathetic educator, 108
classroom management, teacher clarity for,
  25–29
classrooms
    demonstrating empathy, 13–14
    learning outside of, 83
    nurturing empathy within, 57–58, 64–65,
      80

clip charts, 38
cognitive empathy, 4, 44. *See also* perspective
  taking
college, focus on, 87–90
common ground in relationship building,
  30–31
communication, nonverbal, 6, 6*f*, 47–48
compassion, implicit empathy in demonstrating, 14
compassion fatigue, 5, 23
consequences, using instead of punishments,
  37–38
consistency
    behavior, effect on, 96
    in relationship building, 31–32
conversations, restorative, 39–40, 61
cooperative learning structures, modeling
  empathy with, 65–67
crisis of empathy, 8–9
curriculum and instructional design, fostering
  culturally empathetic
    bridge emotional empathy and perspective
      taking with identity charts, 54–56, 55*f*
    build emotional empathy through litera-
      ture, 52
    generate behavioral empathy with prob-
      lem-based learning and STEM, 59–61
    increase perspective taking with artistic
      expression, 56–59
cyclical trauma, 30

dad jokes number talk, 82–83
data collection, 7*f*, 107–108, 109*f*
deficit model of education, 44–46
differentiation, student-driven, 16

discipline
    consequences instead of punishments,
        37–38
    eliminating trauma triggers vs., 24–25
    lowering grades to punish behavior, 96

educator, steps to become an empathetic
    celebrate, 110
    choose strategies, 108
    determine success criteria, 107–108
    identify your motivation, 105, 106f
    introduction, 104–105
    monitor growth, 108, 110
    set your goals, 105–107, 109f
    take baseline data, 107–108, 109f
    use checklists, 108
The Educator's Empathy Checklist, 3f
emotional empathy
    bridging perspective taking with identity
        charts, 54–56, 55f
    building through literature, 52
emotional intelligence, 13
empathic capacity, 5, 54, 63–64
empathic concern, 4
empathic skills, developing, 3, 8–9, 57–58,
    63–64, 104–105
empathy
    defined, 3
    demonstrated, 5–7
    fostering, 11
    genuine, 13–14
    in-group bias for, 8–9
    innate ability for, 8
    lacking, results of, 13
    mirror neurons role in, 5–6
    modeling, 65–67
    teacher clarity engendering, 16–17, 21f
    types of, 3–4, 44
empathy, types of
    affective, 3–4, 44
    behavioral, 4–5, 44, 59–61
    cognitive, 4, 44
empathy and education, Google results for, 1
Empathy Assessment, 2f
Empathy Self-Reflection, 2f
equity, actualizing through empathy
    acknowledge the elephant in the room,
        47–51
    focus on strengths, not deficits, 44–46, 46f
    intention and response in, 61, 62f
    see people as individuals first, 44
    vignette, 49–51
equity efforts in schools, 43, 49–51
extrinsic motivation
    cumulative effect of, 35–36
    intrinsic vs., 35–36
    for repressing feelings, 33

feedback, 70
feelings
    allowing and validating, 32–33, 65
    identifying and redirecting, 32–33, 34f
flexible grouping, 71–73, 72–74f, 75

goal-setting, becoming an empathetic educator,
    105–107, 109f
grading and reporting practices
    background, 90–91
    focus on college, 87–90
    historically, 96
    kindergarten deadlines, 91
    lowering grades to punish behavior, 96
    mixing behavior and academic perfor-
        mance, 95
    report cards, 92–93
    shame from, 15
grading and reporting practices, empathetic
    create learning intentions and success cri-
        teria for student skills, 96–97, 98f
    create non-negotiable grading principles,
        96, 97f
    examples of, 96
    individual growth vs. comparing to others,
        91
    remove judgment and competitive factor,
        92
    report progress in real time, 92–93, 94f,
        95f
    student ownership of their data, 92
    vignette, 99–102
grouping, flexible, 71–73, 72–74f, 75
guilt, 37

identity, defined, 54
identity charts, 54–56, 55f
in-group bias, 8–9
instructional planning, empathetic
    build emotional empathy through litera-
        ture, 52
    generate behavioral empathy with prob-
        lem-based learning and STEM, 59–61
    identity charts to bridge emotional empa-
        thy and perspective taking, 54–56, 55f
    increase perspective taking with artistic
        expression, 56–59
    lacking, example of, 14–15
    learning intentions and success criteria in,
        16–17, 18–21f
    purpose in, 13–14
instruction and assessment, strategies nurturing
    empathy
    flexible grouping, 71–73, 72–74f, 75
    formative assessment, 69–71
    modeling empathy, 65–67
    self-reflection, 64–65, 66f, 69f

instruction and assessment, strategies nurturing empathy (*continued*)
  shared experiences, 80–86
  spaced practice, 75–77
  time is not a success criteria, 77–79
intergenerational trauma, 30
intrinsic motivation, 35–36

judgment, shame and, 9–10

kindergarten deadlines, 91

learning environments, creating empathetic basis for, 17
  consequences instead of punishments, 37–38
  create belonging by building relationships, 29–32
  eliminate trauma triggers, 24–25, 26f
  guideposts for, 23
  intrinsic motivation not extrinsic rewards, 35–36
  promote feelings, 32–33, 34f
  restorative conversations, 39–40
  self-care, 23–24, 42, 42f
learning intentions and success criteria
  in empathetic instructional planning, 16–17, 19–21f
  examples of, 53f, 54f
  grading and reporting practices, empathetic, 97, 98f
  nonacademic example of, 17, 18f
  in student-driven differentiation, 16–17
  Teacher Clarity Checklist, 21f
listening in relationship building, 32
literature, building emotional empathy through, 52
logical consequences, 38

magic bag number talk, 80–82
marginalized groups, acknowledging, 48–49
mass practice, 75–77
microaggressions, 47
Milgram experiment, 13
mirror neurons, 5–6
Mood Meter app, 33
motivation. *See also* extrinsic motivation
  in becoming an empathetic educator, 105, 106f
  grades and, 95
  intrinsic, 35–36
music, increasing perspective taking with, 57

natural consequences, 37–38
nonverbal empathetic behavior, 6, 6f, 7f
Nonverbal Empathy Checklist, 6f
nurturing, 63–65

othering
  identifying in the classroom, 62f
  subgroups, comparing to white norms, 44
  us vs. them, changing, 83
others
  empathizing with, 44
  mirror neurons in perception of, 6
  out-grouping, 9
out-grouping others, 9

perspective taking
  artistic expression in increasing, 56–59
  bridging emotional empathy with identity charts, 54–56, 55f
  explained, 4
pineapple chart, 45
pity, 92
problem-based learning to generate behavioral empathy, 59–61
punishment, consequences instead of, 37–38. *See also* discipline

read-alouds, modeling empathy with, 65–67
relationships. *See also* student-teacher relationships
  restorative conversations in repairing, 39–40, 61
  student-senior citizen, 83
report cards, 92–93
respect, students' experience of, 30
Reverse Pineapple Chart, 45, 46f
rewards. *See* extrinsic motivation

self-care, importance of, 23–24, 42, 42f
self-empathy, practicing, 65
self-esteem, 29
self-perpetuating trauma, 30
self-reflection, 66f, 69f
self-reflection, empathy, 2f, 64–65, 66f, 69f
shame
  avoiding, 28, 47
  causes of, 28
  changing behavior using, 37
  damage caused by, 37
  deficit, 45
  defined, 9
  empathy in creating, 10
  experience of, 10
  guilt vs., 37
  instructional, examples of, 14–15, 16f
  judgment and, 9–10
  learned, 47–48, 89
  learning, 14
  microaggressions and, 47
  mitigating, 11
  root of, 54
  success and, 71, 77

shame (*continued*)
    in trauma victims, 28
    weaponized, 9
shame resilience, 10–11, 49
shaming
    by undeserved rewards, 92
    grades used for, 96
    identity, 89
    implicit, 88
    repairing, 39–40, 61
social-emotional
    component, 85
    issues, 56
    learning (SEL), ix, x, 51, 63, 96
    needs, 64, 107
    skills, x, 36
    success, 78
    supports, 51
soft skills, separating academic progress from, 96
spaced practice, 75–77
Speaking Exchange Project, 83
STEM, generating behavioral empathy, 59–61
strengths, focusing on for equity, 44–46, 46f
students
    ownership of their data, 92
    traumatized, 22, 24–25
student-teacher relationships
    assessment in establishing, 84–86
    cultivating a sense of belonging by build-
        ing, 29–32
    restorative conversations in, 39–40

substance abuse, traumatic experiences and,
    33
success, shame and, 71, 77
success criteria. *See also* learning intentions and
    success criteria
    in becoming an empathetic educator,
        107–108
    importance of, 17
    time as a, 77–79

teacher clarity
    for classroom management, 25–29
    engendering empathy, 16–17, 21f
Teacher Clarity Checklist, 21f
threat precluding empathy, 8
tracking, 73
trauma
    cyclical, 30
    defined, 22
    empathy engendered by, 30
    intergenerational, 30
    self-perpetuating, 30
    students experiencing, 22–23, 24–25
    substance abuse and, 33
trauma triggers
    adverse reactions from, 24–25
    eliminating, 24–25, 26f
    through the lens of empathy, 26f, 27
trauma victims, shame carried by, 28

Video Observation Data Collection Tool, 7f

About the Author

Lisa Westman is an author, speaker, and consultant who works regularly with school systems internationally to provide professional learning on student-driven differentiation, empathy as the foundation of our instructional practices, standards-based learning, and implementing instructional coaching programs. Her presentations are designed to "keep it real," focusing on specific models and strategies that all educators can implement—and, more important, want to implement. She is passionate about teaching and learning, and she is dedicated to inspiring change that helps both students and educators.

She has 17 years of experience as a middle school teacher in gifted humanities, English language arts, and social studies and as an instructional coach specializing in differentiation. She holds a master's degree in teaching from National-Louis University; a bachelor's degree in history and sociology from the University of Illinois at Chicago; and additional endorsements in gifted education, language arts, social studies, and middle school.

Her publications include *Student-Driven Differentiation: 8 Steps to Harmonize Learning in the Classroom* (Corwin Press, 2018) and frequent contributions to *Education Update, Education Week, Education Week Teacher,* and *Edutopia.*

She is married to an educator and is the parent of a 9th grader, a 6th grader, an 8-year-old Pomeranian rat terrier, and an 18-month-old Border Collie. She enjoys the Bar Method and loves music and the city of Chicago.

Photo credit: @chicagophotoart

Related ASCD Resources: Social and Emotional Learning

At the time of publication, the following resources were available (ASCD stock numbers in parentheses):

All Learning Is Social and Emotional: Helping Students Develop Essential Skills for Classroom and Beyond by Nancy Frey, Douglas Fisher, and Dominique Smith (#119033)

The Burnout Cure by Chase Mielke (#119004)

Compassionate Coaching: How to Help Educators Navigate Barriers to Professional Growth by Kathy Perret & Kenny McKee (#121017)

Creating a Trauma-Sensitive Classroom (Quick Reference Guide) by Kristin Souers and Pete Hall (#QRG118054)

The Formative Five: Fostering Grit, Empathy, and Other Success Skills Every Student Needs by Thomas Hoerr (#116043)

Fostering Resilient Learners: Strategies for Create a Trauma-Sensitive Classroom by Kristin Souers with Pete Hall (#116014)

From Behaving to Belonging: The Inclusive Art of Supporting Students Who Challenge Us by Julie Causton and Kate MacLeod (#121011)

Improve Every Lesson Plan with SEL by Jeffrey Benson (#121057)

Integrating SEL into Everyday Instruction (Quick Reference Guide) by Nancy Frey, Dominique Smith, and Douglas Fisher (#QRG119030)

Mindfulness in the Classroom: Strategies for Promoting Concentration, Compassion, and Calm by Thomas Armstrong (#120018)

Relationship, Responsibility, and Regulation: Trauma-Invested Practices for Fostering Resilient Learners by Kristin Souers with Pete Hall (#119027)

So Each May Soar: The Principles and Practices of Learner-Centered Classrooms by Carol Ann Tomlinson (#118006)

Social-Emotional Learning and the Brain: Strategies to Help Your Students Thrive by Marilee Sprenger (#121010)

Teaching to Strengths: Supporting Students Living with Trauma, Violence, and Chronic Stress by Debbie Zacarian, Lourdes Alvarez-Ortiz, and Judie Haynes (#117035)

Trauma-Invested Practices to Meet Students' Needs (Quick Reference Guide) by Kristin Van Marter Souers and Pete Hall (#QRG119077)

For up-to-date information about ASCD resources, go to www.ascd.org. You can search the complete archives of *Educational Leadership* magazine at www.ascd.org/el.

For more information, send an email to member@ascd.org; call 1-800-933-2723 or 1-703-578-9600; send a fax to 1-703-575-5400; or write to Information Services, ASCD, 1703 N. Beauregard St., Alexandria, VA 22311-1714 USA.